D0582165

SELECT WORKS OF POPE

SATIRES AND EPISTLES

OXFORD UNIVERSITY PRESS
AMEN HOUSE, E.C. 4
LONDON EDINBURGH GLASGOW
LEIPZIG NEW YORK TORONTO
MELBOURNE CAPETOWN BOMBAY
CALCUTTA MADRAS SHANGHAI
HUMPHREY MILFORD
PUBLISHER TO THE
UNIVERSITY

POPE

SATIRES AND EPISTLES

EDITED BY

MARK PATTISON, B.D.

SOMETIME RECTOR OF LINCOLN COLLEGE, OXFORD

STEREOTYPE EDITION, CORRECTED

OXFORD
AT THE CLARENDON PRESS

NOTE

In this edition, the *Imitations of Horace*, with the *Epistle to Arbuthnot* and the two *Epilogues*, are, to avoid confusion, numbered continuously with the collective title *Satires and Epistles*.

Title in this Edition.			*Original Title.*	*Date of Publication.*
Satires and Epistles.		Prologue.	Epistle to Dr. Arbuthnot.	1735
„	„	I.	First Satire of Second Book of Horace imitated.	1733
„	„	II.	Second Satire of Second Book of Horace imitated.	1734
„	„	III.	First Epistle of First Book of Horace imitated.	1737
„	„	IV.	Sixth Epistle of First Book of Horace imitated.	1737
„	„	V.	First Epistle of Second Book of Horace imitated	1737
„	„	VI.	Second Epistle of Second Book of Horace imitated.	1737
„	Epilogue	I. }	One Thousand seven Hundred and Thirty-eight.	
„	Epilogue	II. }	Dialogue I. and II.	1738

The imitation of Horace I. Satire 2, is not here given. A few other necessary omissions are indicated by asterisks.

Impression of 1931

First edition, 1872

PRINTED IN GREAT BRITAIN AT THE UNIVERSITY PRESS, OXFORD
BY JOHN JOHNSON, PRINTER TO THE UNIVERSITY

INTRODUCTORY.

THE pieces collected in this volume were published by Pope singly, at various times during the five years from 1733 to 1738. When his Works were first collected, they were placed together in one volume, and entitled *Satires and Epistles of Horace imitated.* It is no paradox to say that these *Imitations* are among the most original of his writings. So entirely do they breathe the spirit of the age and country in which they were written, that they can be read without reference to the Latin model.

Our pleasure indeed is enhanced, and our admiration of the poetic skill raised, when we compare them with Horace, and note the ingenuity with which the English analogue is substituted in every instance for the Roman original. It may be said to be a perfect translation, the persons and things being transferred as well as the words. All translation from an ancient into a modern language involves some modernisation of the idea. It is the problem constantly before the translator, how far he shall carry this transformation. In the early part of the eighteenth century, many of the classical poets suffered translation into English verse upon this system. The aim was to modernise as much as possible. Dryden's *Virgil* and Pope's *Homer* were only attempts to bring Virgil and Homer not only into the language of the 'Town,' but into its modes of thought and expression. The translator followed the precedent of the stage, on which the Greek and Roman heroes appeared in perruque and silk stockings, the court dress of Versailles. In vain Boileau ridiculed the fashion, and (*Art Poétique,* 3. 118) forbade the dramatist 'peindre Caton galant, et Brutus dameret.' The limits of translation and imitation were not distinctly defined.

Oldham translated some Satires of Juvenal on this system; Dryden himself calls his *Art of Poetry* a translation of Boileau, though he has substituted English authors throughout for the French examples. And in his translation of Juvenal, Dryden could not resist introducing Shadwell's name. But Rochester (died 1680), in what he calls an *Allusion to the tenth Sat. of first Book of Horace*, had furnished the first regular example of that style which Pope brought to perfection in these Imitations.

To Lord Bolingbroke Pope assigns (Spence, *Anecdotes*, p. 297) the suggestion of these Imitations, as he did the suggestion of the *Essay on Man.* If the suggestion came from Bolingbroke, the idea was not original. Examples lay everywhere at hand in both French and English. Pope, who himself quotes Creech's Horace (*Sat. and Ep.* 4. 4), could not have been ignorant of what Creech tells his readers, that the same suggestion had been made to him (1684), and rejected in favour of the system of close translation. But Pope may naturally have wished to come forward as a satirist under the shield of a noble name. He seems to feel that the bitter personalities which he is writing may need some such cover. Boileau, before Pope, had felt himself compelled to publish an apology for being a professed satirist. The *Discours sur la Satire* (1668) rests his defence on classical precedent. Because Persius and Juvenal wrote satire without alarming the jealousy of Nero or Trajan, he may follow their example under the milder government of Louis the Great. The monarch treated it as a joke, so no subject had ground for making it a serious offence.

> ' Hier, dit-on, de vous on parla chez le roi,
> Et d'attentat horrible on traita la satyre;
> Et le roi que dit-il? Le roi se prit à rire.'
> Boileau, *Épître*, 6. 52.

So Pope would fain shelter himself under a minister, or, greater name, under Bolingbroke. Of his *Satires of Donne versified* (1735) he tells the reader that they were done at the desire of the Earl of Oxford and the Duke of Shrewsbury; and he does not omit to add that it was while Oxford was Lord Treasurer, and the Duke had been Secretary of State (see *Advertisement* to *Sat. and Ep.* i. p. 37). The tone of this *Advertisement* is apologetic. He endeavours in it to draw a distinction between satire and libel, like a man who began to suspect himself of having been guilty of the latter. 'There is not,' he says, 'in the world a greater error than that which fools are so apt to fall into, and knaves with good reason to encourage, the mistaking a satirist for a libeller; whereas to a true satirist nothing is so odious as a libeller, for the same reason as to a man truly virtuous nothing is so hateful as a hypocrite.'

The distinction which Pope here insists upon, he never observed in his own practice. His more elaborate portraits are so many virulent and abusive lampoons. In his savage assaults on Lady Mary Wortley Montagu, and on Lord Hervey, he passed the bounds of the rules of decorum recognised, not to say in refined, but in decent society. His verses on Addison violate only truth and good feeling. But it is not only in his individual portraits that he is carried beyond the limits of civility, his whole satire is pitched in a key which good taste is compelled to disown. It is trenchant and direct. It does not play, but wound. It is not merely caustic, it is venomous. It betrays a spiteful purpose in the satirist.

Of this fault there were two principal causes; one in the manners of the age, the other in the temperament of the poet.

1. A writer who, like Pope, treats social and personal themes must do so in the tone of the society for which he writes. All poetry, in the time of Pope, was written not for the country, but for the 'Town.' Even the *Essay on Man* reflects, in its subject, the theological turn of coffee-house discussion. The *Satires and Epistles* keep still closer to the tone and topics of London conversation. All the evidence we have goes to shew that in the reign of George II. the finer and more delicate graces did not flourish, or were dying out. The passions of political party occupied all minds. At no period since the great Civil War had the spirit of faction so possessed the English nation. Everything else merged in it. The violence of the

parliamentary struggle engendered a violence of language which lost in refinement what it gained in energy. The character of the great ministerial leader, Sir Robert Walpole, resolute, clear-sighted, and with a thorough knowledge of the world, but coarse, vulgar, and without tincture of letters or culture, is typical of the men by whom he was supported and opposed. Learning was at the lowest ebb. Art existed as portrait-painting or caricature. Literature was a mere arena of partisan warfare. Poetry had degenerated into rhymed pamphlets. The public, barbarised by the gladiatorial spectacle of politics, could relish nothing but blows, and blows were then most applauded when they drew blood. It was impossible that Pope, who desired popularity, should escape the infection. He accordingly wrote *Satires;* or, if he wrote *Epistles* or *Essays,* they were satires only not in name. And in his satire there was no occasion for him to respect the feelings of his enemies, for no one else thought of doing so. The only justification of Pope's outrageous personalities is, that such was the habitual dialect of the contemporary press. And the press only followed the lead of general conversation. In 1720 it was one of the good effects of the South Sea mania that it diverted the talk of the town from the fury of politics. Digby writes (*D. to Pope,* 9 July, 1720), 'The London language and conversation is, I find, quite changed since I left it only three months ago. . . . . I hope this will calm all party rage, and introduce more humanity than has of late prevailed in conversation.' It was sufficient to belong to the Court party to earn a stinging couplet from Pope's pen. His praise was equally blind, for it is bestowed on all Tories, or the Country party as they began to call themselves, without distinction. The *Satires* were so far of external origin. They were not prompted by the 'satiric heart,' but by the prevailing fashion of the Walpolian era, the fashion of unrestrained invective. Pope was conscious of a talent for caustic effects, conscious that he could do better than any one what every one else was doing—sting with epigram.

2. A second and concurrent cause of Pope's satirical poetry

is to be found in the personal temperament and situation of the poet. On this point conflicting opinions have been advanced by critics and editors. While some consider Pope as a malignant libeller, others have treated his satirical language as a mere current form of literature, one of his many affectations. Either of these views appears to be too general and absolute.

It must be allowed that Pope is not animated by the genuine passion of the social reformer, the burning indignation against wrong and baseness of which Juvenal is often taken as the type. 'Pope was contented enough (De Quincey, *Works*, vol. ix. p. 21) with society as he found it; bad it might be, but it was good enough for him. It was the merest self-delusion if, at any moment, the instinct of glorying in his satiric mission persuaded him that in his case it might be said, "facit indignatio versum." Pope having no internal principle of wrath boiling in his breast, being really in the most pacific and charitable frame of mind towards all scoundrels whatsoever, was a hypocrite when he conceited himself to be in a dreadful passion with offenders as a body.' Nor was he the cynic or misanthrope soured, like Swift, by disappointment, or goaded, like Churchill, by hard labour. Pope had not a bad heart. His filial piety and steadiness in his friendships are publicly attested, and his many private charities are equally well ascertained. But what Lord Chesterfield said of him (*Characters*) was equally true, 'he was the most irritable of the *genus irritabile*.' You could never tell what would affront him, and he brooded over particular affronts, scheming revenge in verse. In such cases he was capable of the malice which thirsts for leaving wounds. All those bitter couplets were not impulse or fashion, but meditated stabs of personal vengeance. Besides, though Pope had been well used by the world, and in return liked the world well enough, we must remember that in the period to which the *Satires and Epistles* belong, he was peculiarly situated with regard to society. *His* world had been gradually narrowed by death and desertion. Pope had identified himself with the Tory party. During the plenitude of Sir Robert Walpole's power, which almost exactly corresponds with the composition of these *Satires* (1732–1738), the Tory party had dwindled into comparative insignificance both in numbers and in consideration. Pope, too, was in personal relations, not with the whole Parliamentary opposition, but a small, and that the least popular, section of it. In 1727 Swift retired in disgust to his Irish exile, and returned no more. Bolingbroke, whom Pope looked up to as to a superior being, was not acceptable to his own party, and greatly to their relief withdrew in 1735 to his retirement in Touraine. The tone of the friends had become that of a party whose game was up. Pope 'despairs of his country,' and in his letters to Lord Marchmont, a young recruit whom the dazzling accomplishments of Bolingbroke had attracted, he writes as if virtue had departed from the earth, or was confined to the circle of friends—to Bolingbroke, Marchmont, Lyttelton and himself. (See *Marchmont Papers*, 2. 219.) In such a position the best judgment becomes clouded, and men readily get to think honour and merit a monopoly of their set. The tone of the *Satires and Epistles* breathes some of the bitterness of a coterie, who glorify themselves and asperse mankind. Wherever in these pieces Pope is more genial, it is in recurrence to a former time, the period of his early prime, his first acquaintance with the 'wits' and the 'great,' with Swift, Harley, and St. John. Though only approaching fifty ('Why will you break the sabbath of my days?' *Sat. and Ep.* 3. 3) Pope was prematurely old, and had not moved forward with his age. The enumeration of his friends (*Sat. and Ep. Prol.* 135) is in the past tense, and is an enumeration of the friends of his youth. The times when he could say, 'I condescend sometimes to call a minister my friend,' were long behind him. Only the bitterness is applicable to his contemporaries. And for all outside his own circle he has nothing but bitterness. Some, indeed, were involved who were no longer living, as Addison and Halifax; but these pieces had been prepared long before. Pope was in no mood now to forgive the dead.

This union of tender reference to a more brilliant past, with bitter jealousy against the successful in the present, is the leading contrast which gives life to Pope's satire. In both, in the cherished memories as in the numerous resentments, he was equally sincere. This gives a reality to his words which satire has often wanted when directed against social follies in general, or abstract vices. In Juvenal's lines on Hannibal or Alexander we are always conscious of the absence of true passion. The indignation is theatrical. It is not so in Pope. There may be occasional passages of mere vague tirade for the sake of sustaining the character of moral censor. But in his satirical touches he is in earnest, and in his most severe couplets most so. Even what seem random generalities are often expressions of his real feeling. This reality cannot be felt by readers who are only slightly acquainted with the poet's history, and who are not aware how thoroughly Pope was penetrated by party passion. He truly believes that the Whigs are ruining the country, that the Court is a nest of sycophants, that the majority in the House of Peers is corrupt, and the City is made up of 'thieves, super-cargos, sharpers, and directors.' The same closely-drawn ties which obscured his judgment and confined his sympathies to a clique, save him from one of the defects to which satire is liable, viz. an universal indignation and undirected invective.

One requisite of satire, that it should be an expression of genuine feeling, and not an assumed indignation, is then found in Pope's satire. Into what a different region this raises his satire, may be seen by a comparison with the satires of his contemporary Young, or of his predecessors Hall and Donne. But it is not enough that the anger should be real, it is further requisite that it should be directed upon proper objects. Pope's expressions of hate and dislike were sincere, but were they just? The answer has been implied in what has been already said. Pope's judgments, whether he is speaking of historical characters or of his contemporaries, are most perverse. His allusions to historical personages in the *Satires and Epistles* are few, but enough to shew that he was ignorant of the existence of a tribunal of history, or of that universal jurisprudence which governs its awards. When he comes to speak of his contemporaries he has no test of merit but the pass-word of his coterie. He professes to lay down as his rule, 'A lash like mine no honest man shall dread.' But then the term 'honest man' is convertible with his own circle of friends. At every one else, from 'vice too high' down to 'Budgel in the Mint,' he aims a shot.

It is essential to forming right judgments of others that we should first know ourselves. He who lives in a state of illusion as to his own character and powers will be sure to underrate those of others. His error in judging himself having its root in vanity, his estimate of others will be governed by the interest his vanity may have in exalting or in humbling them. Pope was the victim of a vanity which was not so much personal as the common stock of his set.

But though Pope's satire is vitiated by personal grudge and party spirit, there is a kind of truth which cannot be denied to it. It is unjust, but not altogether untrue. Though all who do not belong to the party are his foes, yet he is 'too discreet to run a-muck and tilt at all he meets.' His fire is not that of artillery which plays on the battalion, but that of the rifle, which picks off its men. It is the condition of human nature that every character, however worthy, has its failings. Pope, with a feeble comprehension of human life as a whole, had a keen eye for these weak places. Here he could be true. This is what makes him so formidable as a satirist. He can pick out all the flaws, all the stains, combine them effectively, and present them as a picture of the man. To his portraits none can deny a certain likeness. They appeal to that weakness in human nature to which La Rochefoucauld's maxim points, that the misfortunes even of our friends are not wholly without something that gratifies us. 'Satire will be heard,' says Gray (*Letters to Walpole*), 'for all the audience are by nature her friends.' Personal malice or party prejudice may have in the first place prompted Pope's onslaught. But where he has selected his victim, he always hits in the weak place. His hate is not blind hate; it only makes him more clear-sighted. He does not accumulate vituperative epithets at random, in the hope, according to the proverb, that 'some will stick,' but finds with ingenious cruelty just the appropriate defect. By this artifice, the greatest and noblest may be made to look mean. Of the great Duke of Marlborough the only trait which Pope records—and he recurs to it—is his love of money. How grand, by contrast, shews Pope's friend, Bolingbroke, who, expressing his admiration of the Duke, when some one present objected his avarice, added, 'He was so great a man, I had almost forgot he had that fault.'

As in many other kinds of art, truth of detail is falsity in general effect. From the nature of satire this is inevitably so. The satirist is bound by his profession to dwell upon the faults. He cannot point out the merits of his characters without disturbing the tone of sentiment to which he appeals. But in drawing character, only the whole truth is the real truth. This even applies to fictitious character as well as to copies of actual life. Porson says (*Rogers' Recollections*, p. 122), 'In drawing a villain we should always furnish him with something that may seem to justify himself to himself.' In one instance only Pope has remembered this rule. In the character of Addison (*Sat. and Ep. Prol.* 193) he has mingled some traits of respect, which set off the imputations, and greatly heighten their effect. The character of Addison is Pope's masterpiece in this kind, because its injustice is artfully veiled under the guise of offended friendship.

Pope has been severely censured for having bestowed so much attention and elaborate verse upon inferior writers, the mere rabble and rout of literature. He called them his 'enemies,' and it is true that they had defamed him. They could not forgive him his success—a success which they had failed in achieving themselves. A distinguished literary success is, like any other success, attended by the envy of the disappointed. But if we condemn the unsuccessful author for the indulgence of a jealousy which it is hard for human nature to stifle, what shall we say of the successful man who turns round upon his yet struggling fellows, insults their misery, and tramples on them, because he has been fortunate enough to emerge? The literary value of the productions of Grub Street may have been little enough, but their authors, as men, were as good and honest men as Pope himself. It is the business of criticism to condemn a bad book. Pope's taste might have been usefully employed, like Boileau's, in signalising pretentious poetry, and exposing ambitious incapacity. But Pope was not content with censuring the books, he attacked their authors. Nor was this mistake enough. He fell furiously upon the trade of authorship, treated poverty as a vice, and descends even to contrast his own 'poet's dignity and ease' with the raggedness and dinnerlessness of the sons of rhyme. Johnson, who had drunk that bitter cup, justly resents this want of feeling. (*Life of Pope.*)

Pope may have caught this tone towards professional authors from his friend the Dean. But he had not Swift's justification; for Swift never derived any pecuniary profit from his writings, with the exception of *Gulliver's Travels*. In Pope it was the more unpardonable, because it was in great part to literary manufacture—to his English Homer—that he owed his own comfortable home. To use his own sarcasm against Addison (*Sat. and Ep. Prol.* 200), he 'hated for arts that caus'd himself to rise.'

The *Dunciad* is the piece which is most obnoxious to this charge. It is wholly inspired by this animosity against needy authors. But the *Satires and Epistles* are not free from the taint. In these we meet with Curll, Cibber, Gildon, Tate, Welsted, Budgell, Eusden, Settle. All these were, as writers, if not below criticism, at least below any criticism that aspired to live. Even if it were not demeaning Pope to notice their productions, it was lessening the chance of his satire being read by posterity. He knew the error he was committing in attaching his verse to such inferior names. He writes to Swift in 1723, 'What Virgil had to do with Mævius that he should wear him on his sleeve to all eternity, I do not know.' That poetry which is to be permanent must deal with permanent themes. Satirical, is not any more than any other, poetry absolved from this obligation. Satire, even when individual, must never lose sight of just and noble ends. Of all petty things nothing is so petty as a petty quarrel. Pope too often allows the personal grudge to be seen through the surface of public police which he puts on his work. He tries to make us think he is descending from a superior sphere to lash scribblers, who had not only sinned against taste by their foolish verses, but had outraged his moral sense by the scandalousness of their lives. He says (again to Swift, 1728), 'As the obtaining the love of valuable men is the happiest end I know of in this life, so the next felicity is to get rid of fools and scoundrels, which was one part of my design in falling upon these authors, whose incapacity is not greater than their insincerity, and of whom I have always found, if I may quote myself, "That each bad author is as bad a friend."' But the thin disguise of offended virtue is too often a cloak for revenge. His most pungent verses can always be referred back to some personal cause of affront—a line in *The Bee*, or a copy of verses upon him which was handed about in manuscript. He knowingly threw away fame to indulge his piques. Compare with this Johnson, of whom it has been said (*Macaulay's Life*), 'A hundred bad writers misrepresented him and reviled him; but not one of the hundred could boast of having been thought by him worthy of a refutation, or even of a retort.'

It is indeed doubtful, and has been doubted with special reference to Pope (by Bowles in his edition), if the attitude of satirist is one which any individual can adopt towards his fellow-men. It is felt to imply an assumption of superiority, moral or intellectual, which can never be possessed by any one man. Even were such infallibility attainable, it would be odious that the possessor of it should himself announce it to the rest of mankind. To this it may be replied, that just as the prophet comes forward to rebuke sin, not in his own name, but in that of the Supreme Judge of the world, so the satirist delivers not his own judgments, but those of society. He enforces the principles of social conduct, or the rules of literary taste, which law does not attempt to cover. He is the organ of public opinion for this duty. (*Quarterly Review*, October 1825.) 'The effect of satire is not confined to daunting vice; virtue feels her confidence increased by being armed with such weapons, and her conscious dignity and scorn augmented in beholding vice publicly humbled. There can be no doubt that Pope's shafts of satire, pointed by wit and winged by verse, have struck on many a heart callous to all but the dread of infamy; and this not merely in the individuals actually exposed, but in all of every age who recognise the same character in themselves, or fear the application of it by others.'

But he who undertakes satire as a public duty must possess an elevation of soul and an impassioned intelligence to which Pope cannot lay claim. Yet Pope had before him two models—models of excellence in very different kinds of satire, but both agreeing in this, that their satire enforced the public reason, and was not the instrument of private vengeance. Pope was well acquainted with the writings of both, but from neither of them could he learn this lesson.

De Quincey has strenuously denied the propriety of denominating Pope and his followers the 'French School.' Without enquiring how far this is true, no student of our poetry can fail to see the influence of Boileau upon Pope's style. In the *Notes* to this edition a number of direct imitations are pointed out. But the resemblance is much more general and diffused than that of single imitations. All that distinguishes Pope from his predecessors of the school of Dryden—his chastized severity of style, as opposed to their florid facility—is due to the example of Boileau. But while thus learning composition from Boileau, Pope neglected to learn what Boileau lays down as the rule of his poetry, ' Rien n'est beau que le vrai.' Boileau is a classic, not only by reason of his style, but in virtue of his judgments. His dicta are so many axioms. When he condemns or commands it is the verdict of common sense that we hear. And Boileau never transgresses the bounds of legitimate criticism. He had no libels on his conscience. He did indeed rouse the wrath of fashionable authors, and of grandees. He refused homage alike to false taste in writing, and to the noble patrons of that false taste. But he did it in tones of manly rebuke, or polished sarcasm. All the forms of eloquent raillery, and well-bred contempt, the keen strokes of wit which it is impossible to parry or to resent, these only are Boileau's weapons. Hence the classic durability of Boileau. His personal allusions are so many principles clothed in concrete form. (*Nisard*, 2. 382.) 'Changez les noms des poëtes immolés par Boileau, sous d'autres noms je vois les mêmes défauts. Les Chapelain, les Scudéry, les Cotin, ne sont si populaires que par ce que les défauts qui se personnifient en eux sont éternels. Tel novateur n'est qu'un vieil ennemi de l'esprit français; il y a près de deux siècles, on le nommait Pradon.' Boileau is consequently a standard at once for the language and the literature of his country. His verdicts are unimpeachable, his decisions without appeal. His *Satires and Epistles* have made, for more than a century, an integral part of all liberal education in France. They do not require the qualifications and abatements which are necessary in putting Pope into the hands of the young.

Another example nearer home was before Pope in Addison, whose pen, in the words of Sainte-Beuve, was 'sans mollesse, et sans amertume.' 'No kind of power (Macaulay, *Essays*, 2. 342) is more formidable than the power of making men ridiculous; and that power Addison possessed in boundless measure. How grossly that power was abused by Swift and by Voltaire is well known. But of Addison it may be confidently affirmed that he has blackened no man's character, nay, that it would be difficult, if not impossible, to find in all the volumes which he has left us a single taunt which can be called ungenerous or unkind. Yet he had detractors; . . . he was a politician; he was the best writer of his party; he lived in times of fierce excitement, in times when persons of high character and station stooped to scurrility such as is now practised only by the basest of mankind. Yet no provocation and no example could induce him to return raillery for raillery.'

These are heavy deductions to make from the merit both of the author and his writings. If these defects are found in Pope, it may be asked—How comes he to be a classic at all, and his poetry to be put forward still as a study, while that of his contemporaries is allowed to fall into oblivion?

The answer has been anticipated in some remarks in Part I. (See *Essay on Man, Introd.*, p. 17.) Pope lives, and must continue to live as long as the English language, by the perfection of his form. Our language is not feeble as a vehicle of emotion, or scanty as a medium of ideas. But it is, in its ordinary employment by our writers, clumsy, cumbrous, without grace, loaded with superfluities, circumlocution, and indirectness. English writers have in general been intent upon some immediate purpose, and have not stayed to finish. In Pope, on the contrary, we have the constant effort to condense, to concentrate meaning. The thought has been turned over and over, till it is brought out finally with a point and finish which themselves elicit admiration. Sometimes, but rarely, does the severity of the writer's taste allow him to overpoint what he wishes to say, and to let the epigram run away with him. If we compare Pope in this respect with our elder writers, even the greatest of them, Shakspeare, Bacon, Taylor, we find them often leaving the track in the pursuit of mere wit—wit which is not subordinate to the general effect, but consists in verbal quibble or far-fetched allusion. Pope's wit is of that perfect kind which does not seem to be sought for its own sake, but to be the appropriate vehicle of the meaning. We are not made to feel that he is constraining himself to write in couplets, but that his couplets are the shape in which he can best make his thoughts tell. He used to say himself that he had found by trial that he could express himself more forcibly in rhyme than in any other form.

Cowper says (*Letters*, Jan. 5, 1782), 'Writers who find it necessary to make such strenuous and painful exertions are generally as phlegmatic as they are correct; but Pope was, in this respect, exempted from the common lot of authors of that class. With the unwearied application of a plodding Flemish painter, who draws a shrimp with the most minute exactness, he had all the genius of one of the first masters. Never, I believe, were such talents and such drudgery united.'

It must not be hence inferred that every line written by Pope is as perfect as it should be, or may be taken as a model. Writing is a sustained endeavour to express meaning, and the artist is perpetually dropping below his own ideal. Besides, a long piece is to be regarded in its effect as a whole. The attempt to make it all point would result in a string of epigrams, not in a complete poem, which must be compounded of complementary parts. Incessant brilliance is unnatural, and fatigues the attention. Pope is at times flat, and below himself; sometimes fails in putting his meaning clearly; is occasionally clumsy; often ungrammatical. But in the art of adjustment of parts, of leading up to the point, of rising and falling, of knowing when to stimulate attention, and when to let it repose, he has few equals in our literature. The failures and the successes of such an artist in language are equally instructive to a learner.

This exquisite skill of literary composition is that which places Pope in the first rank of English classics. But over and above the workmanship, the materials of the *Satires and Epistles* are not without qualities of permanent value. These enduring qualities may be referred to two heads.

1. The social ideas expressed, and the ethical standard implied, have the character of universality. The grave defects we have found in Pope's conception of life, and of human nature, will not allow him to be classed among the leading minds of his country. But though wanting himself the breadth of the highest genius, he lived in an age which was prepared and accustomed to have the understanding appealed to rather than the passions. This will become more intelligible by contrasting Pope with our elder writers generally.

In our elder writers, from the Elizabethan age downwards, is found a wealth of imagery and a compass of language, by the side of which Pope seems at first sight impoverished. Yet none of our poets of the sixteenth and seventeenth centuries, Milton alone excepted, have left works which can pass down to all time as classics of the language. They revel in an exuberant lawlessness of thought as well as of words. They are full of genius, but destitute of that art which alone can make genius tell. Their ideas follow no law, they are whimsical, fanciful, individual. They do not appeal to the universal human sentiment, but to some 'idola tribus.' Pope indeed wrote for his contemporaries, and 'for the Town,' and his *Satires and Epistles* teem with personal allusions. But reason is dominant throughout. These special cases are all brought up for judgment before that common sense which belongs to no age or country, but must be equally accepted by all. Indeed, the progress of cultivation consists in the ascendency gradually acquired by the intellectual associations over the suggestions of personal feeling. Pope's special judgments are constantly at fault, because he is biased by personal spite, or party zeal. But the law under which he is compelled to pronounce judgment is the law of universal reason. He is in our poetry what Boileau is in French (Nisard, *Lit. Franç.* 2. 294), 'the type of the spirit of discipline and choice, of law and proportion, of the effort to raise the idea to its highest degree of generality. This ideal is one towards which all the great writers of the seventeenth century (in France) aspired. Descartes, Pascal, the Port Royal, the *Académie* have all recognised this universality as the supreme law of good writing.'

2. Pope's *Satires and Epistles* have a value for us as a contemporary record, inasmuch as they present the characters and reflect the manners of the period. In this respect they are a composite result of a retrospective sentiment reacting against the poet's actual position. The days of Queen Anne are in Pope's mind, the personages of the court of George II. and Caroline under his pen. Pope's *Satires and Epistles* certainly do not equal Lord Hervey's *Memoirs* in truth, or fulness and development of detail. But they stand next to those *Memoirs* as a lively picture of a section of social life between 1730–40. Lord Hervey presents us with the Court interior, Pope with the literary and opposition side of London life. All this would have been lost to us if Pope, like Bishop Hall in his *Satires*, had satirised abstract vices, or abused fictitious characters.

It has been made a question if all the names in these *Satires*

and Epistles are those of historical or actual persons. The principal ground for doubt is found in Pope's own words (*Satires and
Epistles*, 1. 42), 'A hundred smart in Timon or in Balaam,' &c.
It is true that in these lines Pope is speaking only of the *Moral
Epistles*, in which some fictitious characters are certainly introduced as illustrations. But really the lines referred to are only
an artifice of Pope to disguise the fact that in Timon he *did*
mean the Duke of Chandos. And we have to set against any
weight which these lines may possess in the question his own
declaration (*Satires and Epistles, Advertisement*, p. 23), ' Many will
know their own pictures in it, there being not a circumstance but
what is true; but I have, for the most part, spared their names,
and they may escape being laughed at, if they please.'

But a more decisive proof that real characters are intended is
an examination in detail of all the personal allusions. These in
the *Satires and Epistles* amount to seventy-five. Of these many
are named without disguise. Of those that are veiled under a
pseudonym, some are so clearly indicated as to leave no room for
doubt. Others are known by a tradition which may be traced up
to the time of publication. There remain a few allusions which
we cannot with certainty identify. (1) All the editors agree in
filling up the blank, *Satires and Epistles*, 2. 122, with the name of
Marlborough, but on what evidence I do not know. (2) In 2. 49,
Mr. Carruthers explains 'Avidien or his wife' of Edward Wortley
Montagu and Lady Mary, an interpretation which appears doubtful, though from the context it cannot be doubted that real persons are intended. (3) In 1. 49, Dr. Bennett affirmed that Lord
Ilchester and Lord Holland were meant. But see note on the
passage. (4) In 4. 87, the 'three ladies' cannot now be identified,
yet Warburton, who himself cannot give the names, gives us to
understand that the allusion was to fact. Other uncertain
references are noticed in their place. It is true of the whole of
Pope's satirical writings that there are very few fancy characters.
So little did he care for playing with shadows, that even the personages in the farce *Three Hours after Marriage* (in which he
assisted Gay and Arbuthnot) represent living persons.

As Pope's pictures, then, are all portraits, it becomes necessary to know something of the characters which are brought upon the stage. It is true that the execution and literary beauties of his verse may be appreciated without this knowledge; yet not then wholly, inasmuch as the appropriateness of the touches is one of the elements of our judgment. But Pope is also a landmark in the literary and social history of England. There has accumulated round Pope's poems a mass of biographical anecdote such as surrounds the writings of no other English author. The student of our literature will find that his enjoyment of the wit of the *Satires and Epistles* is increased exactly in proportion as he extends his knowledge of the period.

It would be useful to begin by reading over a summary of the public events of the reign of George II. For this purpose, Lord Stanhope's *History of England* offers a convenient and elegant abridgment. Mr. Carruthers' *Life of Pope*, 2nd edition, 1858, will be found to embody in an interesting narrative most of the ascertained facts about the poet and his works. For more complete information, the *Memoirs*, and other publications of the time, referred to in the *Notes* at the end of this volume should be consulted. Nothing further has been attempted in these *Notes* than to indicate to the student the sources of illustration. He should in no case rest satisfied with the information the *Notes* afford. They are a mere key to the explanatory literature, and not a substitute for it.

Pope's orthography is careless and inconsistent. Not only proper names, but ordinary words, are spelt in different ways at different times. But in this also he was the man of his age. It may be a question if his errors should be corrected. But it cannot be right to reduce the orthography of 1730–40 to the conventional standard now established. The text therefore of Warburton's ed. 1751 has been scrupulously retained, errors, press or clerical, alone excepted.

M. P.

LINCOLN COLLEGE,
    January, 1872.

SATIRES AND EPISTLES.

PROLOGUE.

An Epistle to Dr. Arbuthnot.

ADVERTISEMENT.

THIS paper is a sort of bill of complaint, begun many years since, and drawn up by snatches, as the several occasions offered. I had no thoughts of publishing it, till it pleased some persons of rank and fortune (the authors of *Verses to the imitator of Horace*, and of an *Epistle to a Doctor of Divinity from a nobleman at Hampton Court*) to attack, in a very extraordinary manner, not only my writings (of which, being public, the public is judge), but my person, morals, and family, whereof, to those who know me not, a truer information may be requisite. Being divided between the necessity to say something of myself, and my own laziness to undertake so aukward a task, I thought it the shortest way to put the last hand to this epistle. If it have anything pleasing, it will be that by which I am most desirous to please, the truth and the sentiment; and if anything offensive, it will be only to those I am least sorry to offend, the vicious or the ungenerous.

Many will know their own pictures in it, there being not a circumstance but what is true; but I have, for the most part, spared their names, and they may escape being laughed at, if they please.

I would have some of them know, it was owing to the request of the learned and candid friend to whom it is inscribed, that I make not as free use of theirs as they have done of mine. However, I shall have this advantage, and honour, on my side, that whereas, by their proceeding, any abuse may be directed at any man, no injury can possibly be done by mine, since a nameless character can never be found out, but by its truth and likeness.

P.

P. HUT, shut the door, good John! fatigu'd I said,
Tye up the knocker, say I'm sick, I'm dead.
The dog-star rages! nay 'tis past a doubt,
All Bedlam, or Parnassus, is let out:

Fire in each eye, and papers in each hand,
They rave, recite, and madden round the land.
    What walls can guard me, or what shades can hide?
They pierce my thickets, thro' my grot they glide,
By land, by water, they renew the charge,
They stop the chariot, and they board the barge.   10
No place is sacred, not the church is free,
Ev'n Sunday shines no Sabbath-day to me:
Then from the Mint walks forth the man of rhyme,
Happy! to catch me, just at dinner-time.
    Is there a parson, much be-mus'd in beer,
A maudlin poetess, a rhyming peer,
A clerk, foredoom'd his father's soul to cross,
Who pens a stanza, when he should engross?
Is there, who, lock'd from ink and paper, scrawls
With desp'rate charcoal round his darken'd walls?   20
All fly to Twit'nam, and in humble strain
Apply to me, to keep them mad or vain.
Arthur, whose giddy son neglects the laws,
Imputes to me and my damn'd works the cause:
Poor Cornus sees his frantic wife elope,
And curses wit, and poetry, and Pope.
    Friend to my life! (which did not you prolong,
The world had wanted many an idle song)
What drop or nostrum can this plague remove?
Or which must end me, a fool's wrath or love?   30
A dire dilemma! either way I'm sped.
If foes, they write, if friends, they read me dead.
Seiz'd and ty'd down to judge, how wretched I!
Who can't be silent, and who will not lye:
To laugh, were want of goodness and of grace,
And to be grave, exceeds all pow'r of face.

I sit with sad civility, I read
With honest anguish, and an aching head;
And drop at last, but in unwilling ears,
This saving counsel, 'Keep your piece nine years.' 40

    Nine years! cries he, who high in Drury-lane,
Lull'd by soft zephyrs thro' the broken pane,
Rhymes ere he wakes, and prints before term ends,
Oblig'd by hunger, and request of friends:
'The piece, you think, is incorrect? why take it,
I'm all submission, what you'd have it, make it.'

    Three things another's modest wishes bound,
My friendship, and a prologue, and ten pound.

    Pitholeon sends to me: 'You know his Grace,
'I want a patron; ask him for a place.' 50
Pitholeon libell'd me—'but here's a letter
Informs you, Sir, 'twas when he knew no better.
Dare you refuse him? Curl invites to dine,
He'll write a journal, or he'll turn divine.'

    Bless me! a packet.—''Tis a stranger sues,
A virgin tragedy, an orphan muse.'
If I dislike it, 'Furies, death and rage!'
If I approve, 'Commend it to the stage.'
There, thank my stars, my whole commission ends,
The players and I, are, luckily, no friends. 60
Fir'd that the house reject him, ''Sdeath I'll print it,
And shame the fools—Your int'rest, Sir, with Lintot.'
Lintot, dull rogue! will think your price too much:
'Not, Sir, if you revise it, and retouch.'
All my demurs but double his attacks;
At last he whispers, 'Do; and we go snacks.'
Glad of a quarrel, strait I clap the door,
Sir, let me see your works and you no more.

'Tis sung, when Midas' ears began to spring,
(Midas, a sacred person and a king)   70
His very minister who spy'd them first,
Some say his queen, was forc'd to speak, or burst.
And is not mine, my friend, a sorer case,
When ev'ry coxcomb perks them in my face?
    A. Good friend forbear! you deal in dang'rous things,
I'd never name queens, ministers, or kings;
Keep close to ears, and those let asses prick,
'Tis nothing—*P.* Nothing? if they bite and kick?
Out with it, Dunciad! let the secret pass,
That secret to each fool, that he's an ass: 80
The truth once told (and wherefore should we lie?)
The queen of Midas slept, and so may I.
    You think this cruel? take it for a rule,
No creature smarts so little as a fool.
Let peals of laughter, Codrus! round thee break,
Thou unconcern'd canst hear the mighty crack:
Pit, box, and gall'ry in convulsions hurl'd,
Thou stand'st unshook amidst a bursting world.
Who shames a scribler? break one cobweb thro',
He spins the slight, self-pleasing thread anew: 90
Destroy his fib or sophistry, in vain,
The creature's at his dirty work again,
Thron'd on the centre of his thin designs,
Proud of a vast extent of flimzy lines!
Whom have I hurt? has poet yet, or peer,
Lost the arch'd eye-brow, or Parnassian sneer?

      *   *   *   *   *   *   *
     *   *   *   *   *   *   *

Does not one table Bavius still admit?
Still to one bishop Philips seem a wit?   100

Still Sappho—*A.* Hold; for God-sake—you'll offend,
No names—be calm—learn prudence of a friend:
I too could write, and I am twice as tall;
But foes like these—*P.* One flatt'rer's worse than all.
Of all mad creatures, if the learn'd are right,
It is the slaver kills, and not the bite.
A fool quite angry is quite innocent:
Alas! 'tis ten times worse when they repent.

One dedicates in high heroic prose,
And ridicules beyond a hundred foes: 110
One from all Grub-street will my fame defend,
And more abusive, calls himself my friend.
This prints my letters, that expects a bribe,
And others roar aloud, ' Subscribe, subscribe.'

There are, who to my person pay their court:
I cough like Horace, and, tho' lean, am short,
Ammon's great son one shoulder had too high,
Such Ovid's nose, and, 'Sir! you have an eye—'
Go on, obliging creatures, make me see
All that disgrac'd my betters, met in me.   120
Say for my comfort, languishing in bed,
' Just so immortal Maro held his head :'
And when I die, be sure you let me know
Great Homer dy'd three thousand years ago.

Why did I write? what sin to me unknown
Dipt me in ink, my parents', or my own?
As yet a child, nor yet a fool to fame,
I lisp'd in numbers, for the numbers came.
I left no calling for this idle trade,
No duty broke, no father disobey'd.   130
The muse but serv'd to ease some friend, not wife,
To help me thro' this long disease, my life,

To second, Arbuthnot! thy art and care,
And teach the being you preserv'd to bear.
   But why then publish? Granville the polite,
And knowing Walsh, would tell me I could write;
Well-natur'd Garth inflam'd with early praise,
And Congreve lov'd, and Swift endur'd my lays;
The courtly Talbot, Somers, Sheffield read,
Ev'n mitred Rochester would nod the head,   140
And St. John's self, great Dryden's friends before,
With open arms receiv'd one poet more.
Happy my studies, when by these approv'd!
Happier their author, when by these belov'd!
From these the world will judge of men and books,
Not from the Burnets, Oldmixons, and Cooks.
   Soft were my numbers; who could take offence
While pure Description held the place of sense?
Like gentle Fanny's was my flow'ry theme,
A painted mistress, or a purling stream.   150
Yet then did Gildon draw his venal quill;
I wish'd the man a dinner, and sate still.
Yet then did Dennis rave in furious fret;
I never answer'd, I was not in debt.
If want provok'd, or madness made them print,
I wag'd no war with Bedlam or the Mint.
   Did some more sober critic come abroad;
If wrong, I smil'd; if right, I kiss'd the rod.
Pains, reading, study, are their just pretence,
And all they want is spirit, taste, and sense.   160
Commas and points they set exactly right,
And 'twere a sin to rob them of their mite.
Yet ne'er one sprig of laurel grac'd these ribalds,
From slashing Bentley down to pidling Tibalds:

Each wight, who reads not, and but scans and spells,
Each word-catcher, that lives on syllables,
Ev'n such small critics some regard may claim,
Preserv'd in Milton's or in Shakespear's name.
Pretty! in amber to observe the forms
Of hairs, or straws, or dirt, or grubs, or worms! 170
The things we know are neither rich nor rare,
But wonder how the devil they got there.

Were others angry: I excus'd them too ;
Well might they rage, I gave them but their due.
A man's true merit 'tis not hard to find ;
But each man's secret standard in his mind,
That casting-weight pride adds to emptiness,
This, who can gratify ? for who can guess ?
The bard whom pilfer'd Pastorals renown,
Who turns a Persian tale for half-a-crown, 180
Just writes to make his barrenness appear,
And strains from hard-bound brains, eight lines a year;
He, who still wanting, tho' he lives on theft,
Steals much, spends little, yet has nothing left:
And he, who now to sense, now nonsense leaning,
Means not, but blunders round about a meaning :
And he, whose fustian's so sublimely bad,
It is not poetry, but prose run mad :
All these, my modest Satire bad translate,
And own'd that nine such poets made a Tate. 190
How did they fume, and stamp, and roar, and chafe !
And swear, not Addison himself was safe.

Peace to all such ! but were there one whose fires
True genius kindles, and fair fame inspires ;
Blest with each talent and each art to please,
And born to write, converse, and live with ease:

Should such a man, too fond to rule alone,
Bear, like the Turk, no brother near the throne,
View him with scornful, yet with jealous eyes,
And hate for arts that caus'd himself to rise;　　200
Damn with faint praise, assent with civil leer,
And without sneering, teach the rest to sneer;
Willing to wound, and yet afraid to strike,
Just hint a fault, and hesitate dislike;
Alike reserv'd to blame, or to commend,
A tim'rous foe, and a suspicious friend;
Dreading ev'n fools, by flatterers besieged,
And so obliging, that he ne'er oblig'd;
Like Cato, give his little senate laws,
And sit attentive to his own applause;　　210
While wits and Templars ev'ry sentence raise,
And wonder with a foolish face of praise—
Who but must laugh, if such a man there be?
Who would not weep, if Atticus were he!

　　What tho' my name stood rubric on the walls,
Or plaister'd posts, * * in capitals?
Or smoking forth, a hundred hawkers' load,
On wings of winds came flying all abroad?
I sought no homage from the race that write;
I kept, like Asian monarchs, from their sight:　　220
Poems I heeded (now be-rhym'd so long)
No more than thou, great George! a birth-day song.
I ne'er with wits or witlings pass'd my days,
To spread about the itch of verse and praise;
Nor like a puppy, daggled thro' the town,
To fetch and carry sing-song up and down;
Nor at rehearsals sweat, and mouth'd, and cry'd,
With handkerchief and orange at my side;

But sick of fops, and poetry, and prate,
To Bufo left the whole Castalian state.   230
　　Proud as Apollo on his forked hill,
Sate full-blown Bufo, puff'd by ev'ry quill;
Fed with soft Dedication all day long,
Horace and he went hand in hand in song.
His library, where busts of poets dead
And a true Pindar stood without a head,
Receiv'd of wits an undistinguish'd race,
Who first his judgment ask'd, and then a place:
Much they extoll'd his pictures, much his seat,
And flatter'd ev'ry day, and some days eat: 240
Till grown more frugal in his riper days,
He paid some bards with port, and some with praise,
To some a dry rehearsal was assign'd,
And others, harder still, he paid in kind.
Dryden alone (what wonder?) came not nigh,
Dryden alone escap'd this judging eye:
But still the great have kindness in reserve,
He help'd to bury whom he help'd to starve.
　　May some choice patron bless each gray goose quill!
May every Bavius have his Bufo still!   250
So when a statesman wants a day's defence,
Or envy holds a whole week's war with sense,
Or simple pride for flatt'ry makes demands,
May dunce by dunce be whistled off my hands!
Blest be the great! for those they take away,
And those they left me; for they left me Gay;
Left me to see neglected genius bloom,
Neglected die, and tell it on his tomb:
Of all thy blameless life the sole return
My verse, and Queensb'ry weeping o'er thy urn!   260

Oh let me live my own, and die so too!
(To live and die is all I have to do:)
Maintain a poet's dignity and ease,
And see what friends, and read what books I please:
Above a patron, tho' I condescend
Sometimes to call a minister my friend.
I was not born for courts or great affairs;
I pay my debts, believe, and say my pray'rs;
Can sleep without a poem in my head,
Nor know, if Dennis be alive or dead.   270

Why am I ask'd what next shall see the light?
Heav'ns! was I born for nothing but to write?
Has life no joys for me? or, to be grave,
Have I no friend to serve, no soul to save?
' I found him close with Swift—Indeed? no doubt
(Cries prating Balbus) something will come out.'
'Tis all in vain, deny it as I will,
' No, such a genius never can lie still;'
And then for mine obligingly mistakes
The first lampoon Sir Will. or Bubo makes.   280
Poor guiltless I! and can I chuse but smile,
When ev'ry coxcomb knows me by my style?

Curst be the verse, how well soe'er it flow,
That tends to make one worthy man my foe,
Give virtue scandal, innocence a fear,
Or from the soft-ey'd virgin steal a tear!
But he who hurts a harmless neighbour's peace,
Insults fall'n worth, or beauty in distress,
Who loves a lye, lame slander helps about,
Who writes a libel, or who copies out: 290
That fop, whose pride affects a patron's name,
Yet absent, wounds an author's honest fame;

Who can your merit selfishly approve,
And show the sense of it without the love;
Who has the vanity to call you friend,
Yet wants the honour, injur'd, to defend;
Who tells whate'er you think, whate'er you say,
And, if he lye not, must at least betray:
Who to the Dean and silver bell can swear,
And sees at Cannons what was never there; 300
Who reads, but with a lust to misapply,
Make satire a lampoon, and fiction lye;
A lash like mine no honest man shall dread,
But all such babbling blockheads in his stead.

Let Sporus tremble—*A.* What? that thing of silk,
Sporus, that mere white curd of ass's milk?
Satire or sense, alas! can Sporus feel?
Who breaks a butterfly upon a wheel?

P. Yet let me flap this bug with gilded wings,
This painted child of dirt, that stinks and stings; 310
Whose buzz the witty and the fair annoys,
Yet wit ne'er tastes, and beauty ne'er enjoys:
So well-bred spaniels civilly delight
In mumbling of the game they dare not bite.
Eternal smiles his emptiness betray,
As shallow streams run dimpling all the way.
Whether in florid impotence he speaks,
And, as the prompter breathes, the puppet squeaks;
Or at the ear of Eve, familiar toad,
Half froth, half venom, spits himself abroad, 320
In puns, or politics, or tales, or lies,
Or spite, or smut, or rhymes, or blasphemies.
His wit all see-saw, between that and this,
Now high, now low, now master up, now miss,
And he himself one vile antithesis.

D

Amphibious thing! that acting either part,
The trifling head, or the corrupted heart,
Fop at the toilet, flatt'rer at the board,
Now trips a lady, and now struts a lord.
Eve's tempter thus the rabbins have exprest,   330
A cherub's face, a reptile all the rest.
Beauty that shocks you, parts that none will trust,
Wit that can creep, and pride that licks the dust.

  Not fortune's worshipper, nor fashion's fool,
Not lucre's madman, nor ambition's tool,
Not proud, nor servile; be one poet's praise,
That, if he pleas'd, he pleas'd by manly ways:
That flatt'ry, ev'n to kings, he held a shame,
And thought a lye in verse or prose the same,
That not in fancy's maze he wander'd long,   340
But stoop'd to truth, and moraliz'd his song:
That not for fame, but virtue's better end,
He stood the furious foe, the timid friend,
The damning critic, half approving wit,
The coxcomb hit, or fearing to be hit;
Laugh'd at the loss of friends he never had,
The dull, the proud, the wicked, and the mad;
The distant threats of vengeance on his head,
The blow unfelt, the tear he never shed;
The tale reviv'd, the lye so oft o'erthrown,   350
Th' imputed trash, and dulness not his own;
The morals blacken'd when the writings 'scape,
The libel'd person, and the pictur'd shape;
Abuse, on all he lov'd, or lov'd him, spread,
A friend in exile, or a father dead;
The whisper, that to greatness still too near,
Perhaps yet vibrates on his sov'reign's ear—

Welcome for thee, fair virtue! all the past:
For thee, fair virtue! welcome ev'n the last!

　A. But why insult the poor, affront the great?　360
P. A knave's a knave, to me, in ev'ry state:
Alike my scorn, if he succeed or fail,
Sporus at court, or Japhet in a jail,
A hireling scribler, or a hireling peer,
Knight of the post corrupt, or of the shire;
If on a pillory, or near a throne,
He gain his prince's ear, or lose his own.

　Yet soft by nature, more a dupe than wit,
Sappho can tell you how this man was bit:
This dreaded sat'rist Dennis will confess　　370
Foe to his pride, but friend to his distress:
So humble, he has knock'd at Tibbald's door,
Has drunk with Cibber, nay has rhym'd for Moor.
Full ten years slander'd, did he once reply?
Three thousand suns went down on Welsted's lye.
To please a mistress one aspers'd his life:
He lash'd him not, but let her be his wife;
Let Budgel charge low Grub-street on his quill,
And write whate'er he pleas'd, except his will;
Let the two Curls of town and court, abuse　　380
His father, mother, body, soul, and muse.
Yet why? that father held it for a rule,
It was a sin to call our neighbour fool:
That harmless mother thought * * * * *:
Hear this, and spare his family, James Moore!
Unspotted names, and memorable long!
If there be force in virtue, or in song.

　Of gentle blood, part shed in honour's cause,
While yet in Britain honour had applause,

Each parent sprung—*A.* What fortune, pray?—
    P. Their own,   390
And better got, than Bestia's from the throne.
Born to no pride, inheriting no strife,
Nor marrying discord in a noble wife,
Stranger to civil and religious rage,
The good man walk'd innoxious thro' his age.
No courts he saw, no suits would ever try,
Nor dar'd an oath, nor hazarded a lye.
Unlearn'd, he knew no schoolman's subtile art,
No language, but the language of the heart.
By nature honest, by experience wise,   400
Healthy by temp'rance, and by exercise;
His life, tho' long, to sickness past unknown,
His death was instant, and without a groan.
O grant me thus to live, and thus to die!
Who sprung from kings shall know less joy than I.

    O friend! may each domestic bliss be thine!
Be no unpleasing melancholy mine:
Me, let the tender office long engage,
To rock the cradle of reposing age,
With lenient arts extend a mother's breath,   410
Make languor smile, and smooth the bed of death,
Explore the thought, explain the asking eye,
And keep a while one parent from the sky!
On cares like these if length of days attend,
May heav'n, to bless those days, preserve my friend,
Preserve him social, chearful, and serene,
And just as rich as when he serv'd a queen.

    A. Whether that blessing be deny'd or giv'n,
Thus far was right, the rest belongs to heav'n.

SATIRES AND EPISTLES.

To Mr. Fortescue.

(HORACE. 2 Sat. 1.)

ADVERTISEMENT.

THE occasion of publishing these Imitations was the clamour rais'd on some
of my Epistles. An answer from Horace was both more full, and of
more dignity, than any I could have made in my own person; and
the example of much greater freedom in so eminent a divine as Dr.
Donne, seem'd a proof with what indignation and contempt a Christian
may treat vice or folly, in ever so low, or ever so high a station. Both
these authors were acceptable to the princes and ministers under whom
they lived. The Satires of Dr. Donne I versified, at the desire of the
Earl of Oxford, while he was Lord Treasurer, and of the Duke of
Shrewsbury, who had been Secretary of State; neither of whom look'd
upon a satire on vicious courts as any reflection on those they serv'd in.
And indeed there is not in the world a greater error, than that which
fools are so apt to fall into, and knaves with good reason to encourage, the
mistaking a satirist for a libeller; whereas to a true satirist nothing
is so odious as a libeller, for the same reason as to a man truly virtuous
nothing is so hateful as a hypocrite.

Uni aequus virtuti atque ejus amicis.

P.

P. HERE are, I scarce can think it, but am told,
There are, to whom my satire seems too bold:
Scarce to wise Peter complaisant enough,
And something said of Chartres much too rough.
The lines are weak, another's pleas'd to say,
Lord Fanny spins a thousand such a day.

Tim'rous by nature, of the rich in awe,
I come to counsel learned in the law:
You'll give me, like a friend both sage and free,
Advice; and, as you use, without a fee.   10

    F. I'd write no more.

                P. Not write? but then I think,
And for my soul I cannot sleep a wink.
I nod in company, I wake at night,
Fools rush into my head, and so I write.

    F. You could not do a worse thing for your life.
Why, if the nights seem tedious—take a wife:
Or rather truly, if your point be rest,
Lettuce and cowslip-wine; probatum est.
But talk with Celsus, Celsus will advise
Hartshorn, or something that shall close your eyes.   20
Or, if you needs must write, write Cæsar's praise,
You'll gain at least a knighthood, or the bays.

    P. What? like Sir Richard, rumbling, rough, and
      fierce,
With arms and George and Brunswick crowd the
      verse,
Rend with tremendous sound your ears asunder,
With gun, drum, trumpet, blunderbuss, and thunder?
Or nobly wild, with Budgel's fire and force,
Paint angels trembling round his falling horse?

    F. Then all your muse's softer art display,
Let Carolina smooth the tuneful lay,   30
Lull with Amelia's liquid name the Nine,
And sweetly flow thro' all the royal line.

    P. Alas! few verses touch their nicer ear;
They scarce can bear their Laureate twice a year;
And justly Cæsar scorns the poet's lays,
It is to history he trusts for praise.

F. Better be Cibber, I'll maintain it still,
Than ridicule all taste, blaspheme quadrille,
Abuse the city's best good men in metre,
And laugh at peers that put their trust in Peter.   40
Ev'n those you touch not, hate you.
                              P. What should ail them?
  F. A hundred smart in Timon and in Balaam:
The fewer still you name, you wound the more;
Bond is but one, but Harpax is a score.
  P. Each mortal has his pleasure: none deny
Scarsdale his bottle, Darty his ham-pye;
Ridotta sips and dances, till she see
The doubling lustres dance as fast as she;
F— loves the senate, Hockley-hole his brother,
Like in all else, as one egg to another.   50
I love to pour out all myself, as plain
As downright Shippen, or as old Montaigne:
In them, as certain to be lov'd as seen,
The soul stood forth, nor kept a thought within;
In me what spots (for spots I have) appear,
Will prove at least the medium must be clear.
In this impartial glass, my muse intends
Fair to expose myself, my foes, my friends;
Publish the present age; but where my text
Is vice too high, reserve it for the next: 60
My foes shall wish my life a longer date,
And ev'ry friend the less lament my fate.
My head and heart thus flowing thro' my quill,
Verse-man or prose-man, term me which you will,
Papist or Protestant, or both between,
Like good Erasmus in an honest mean,
In moderation placing all my glory,
While Tories call me Whig, and Whigs a Tory.

Satire's my weapon, but I'm too discreet
To run a-muck, and tilt at all I meet;   70
I only wear it in a land of Hectors,
Thieves, supercargoes, sharpers and directors.
Save but our army! and let Jove incrust
Swords, pikes, and guns, with everlasting rust!
Peace is my dear delight—not Fleury's more:
But touch me, and no minister so sore.
Whoe'er offends, at some unlucky time
Slides into verse, and hitches in a rhyme,
Sacred to ridicule his whole life long,
And the sad burthen of some merry song.   80

Slander or poison dread from Delia's rage,
Hard words or hanging, if your judge be Page.
From furious Sappho scarce a milder fate,

    *   *   *   *   *   *

Its proper pow'r to hurt, each creature feels;
Bulls aim their horns, and asses lift their heels;
'Tis a bear's talent not to kick, but hug;
And no man wonders he's not stung by pug.
So drink with Walters, or with Chartres eat,
They'll never poison you, they'll only cheat.   90

Then, learned Sir! (to cut the matter short)
Whate'er my fate, or well or ill at court,
Whether old age, with faint but chearful ray,
Attends to gild the ev'ning of my day,
Or death's black wing already be display'd,
To wrap me in the universal shade;
Whether the darken'd room to muse invite,
Or whiten'd wall provoke the skew'r to write:
In durance, exile, Bedlam, or the Mint,
Like Lee or Budgel, I will rhyme and print.   100

F. Alas young man! your days can ne'er be long,
In flow'r of age you perish for a song!
Plums and directors, Shylock and his wife,
Will club their testers, now, to take your life!

P. What? arm'd for virtue when I point the pen,
Brand the bold front of shameless guilty men;
Dash the proud gamester in his gilded car;
Bare the mean heart that lurks beneath a star;
Can there be wanting, to defend her cause,
Lights of the Church, or guardians of the laws?   110
Could pension'd Boileau lash in honest strain
Flatt'rers and bigots ev'n in Louis' reign?
Could Laureate Dryden pimp and fry'r engage,
Yet neither Charles nor James be in a rage?
And I not strip the gilding off a knave,
Unplac'd, unpension'd, no man's heir, or slave?
I will, or perish in the gen'rous cause:
Hear this and tremble! you, who 'scape the laws.
Yes, while I live, no rich or noble knave
Shall walk the world, in credit, to his grave.   120
To virtue only and her friends a friend,
The world beside may murmur, or commend.
Know, all the distant din that world can keep,
Rolls o'er my grotto, and but sooths my sleep.
There, my retreat the best companions grace,
Chiefs out of war, and statesmen out of place.
There St. John mingles with my friendly bowl
The feast of reason and the flow of soul:
And he, whose lightning pierc'd th' Iberian lines,
Now forms my quincunx, and now ranks my vines,
Or tames the genius of the stubborn plain,   131
Almost as quickly as he conquer'd Spain.

Envy must own, I live among the great,
No pimp of pleasure, and no spy of state,
With eyes that pry not, tongue that ne'er repeats,
Fond to spread friendships, but to cover heats;
To help who want, to forward who excel;
This, all who know me, know; who love me, tell;
And who unknown defame me, let them be
Scriblers or peers, alike are mob to me.   140
This is my plea, on this I rest my cause—
What saith my counsel, learned in the laws?

    F. Your plea is good; but still I say, beware!
Laws are explain'd by men—so have a care.
It stands on record, that in Richard's times
A man was hang'd for very honest rhymes;
Consult the statute, quart. I think, it is,
Edwardi sext. or prim. et quint. Eliz.
See ' Libels, Satires '—here you have it—read.

    P. Libels and satires! lawless things indeed!   150
But grave Epistles, bringing vice to light,
Such as a king might read, a bishop write,
Such as Sir Robert would approve—

                       F. Indeed?
The case is alter'd—you may then proceed;
In such a cause the plaintiff will be hiss'd,
My lords the judges laugh, and you're dismiss'd.

SATIRES AND EPISTLES

II.

To Mr. Bethel.

(Horace, 2 Sat. 2.)

WHAT, and how great, the virtue and the art
To live on little with a chearful heart;
(A doctrine sage, but truly none of mine)
Let's talk, my friends, but talk before we dine.
Not when a gilt buffet's reflected pride
Turns you from sound philosophy aside;
Not when from plate to plate your eye-balls roll,
And the brain dances to the mantling bowl.
   Hear Bethel's sermon, one not vers'd in
      schools,
But strong in sense, and wise without the rules. 10
   Go work, hunt, exercise ! he thus began,
Then scorn a homely dinner, if you can.
Your wine lock'd up, your butler stroll'd abroad,
Or fish deny'd (the river yet unthaw'd)
If then plain bread and milk will do the feat,
The pleasure lies in you, and not the meat.
   Preach as I please, I doubt our curious men
Will chuse a pheasant still before a hen;
Yet hens of Guinea full as good I hold,
Except you eat the feathers green and gold. 20

Of carps and mullets why prefer the great,
(Tho' cut in pieces ere my lord can eat)
Yet for small turbots such esteem profess?
Because God made these large, the other less.
Oldfield with more than harpy throat endu'd,
Cries 'Send me, gods! a whole hog barbecu'd!'
Oh blast it, south-winds! till a stench exhale
Rank as the ripeness of a rabbit's tail.
By what criterion do you eat, d'ye think,
If this is priz'd for sweetness, that for stink?   30
When the tir'd glutton labours thro' a treat,
He finds no relish in the sweetest meat,
He calls for something bitter, something sour,
And the rich feast concludes extremely poor:
Cheap eggs, and herbs, and olives still we see;
Thus much is left of old simplicity!
The robin-red-breast till of late had rest,
And children sacred held a martin's nest,
Till beccaficos sold so dev'lish dear
To one that was, or would have been, a peer.   40
Let me extol a cat, on oysters fed,
I'll have a party at the Bedford-head;
Or ev'n to crack live crawfish recommend;
I'd never doubt at court to make a friend.
    'Tis yet in vain, I own, to keep a pother
About one vice, and fall into the other.
Between excess and famine lies a mean;
Plain, but not sordid; tho' not splendid, clean.
    Avidien, or his wife (no matter which,
For him you'll call a dog, and her a bitch)   50
Sell their presented partridges, and fruits,
And humbly live on rabbits and on roots:

One half-pint bottle serves them both to dine,
And is at once their vinegar and wine.
But on some lucky day (as when they found
A lost bank bill, or heard their son was drown'd)
At such a feast, old vinegar to spare,
Is what two souls so gen'rous cannot bear:
Oyl, tho' it stink, they drop by drop impart,
But sowse the cabbage with a bounteous heart.   60

He knows to live, who keeps the middle state,
And neither leans on this side, nor on that;
Nor stops, for one bad cork, his butler's pay,
Swears, like Albutius, a good cook away;
Nor lets, like Nævius, ev'ry error pass,
The musty wine, foul cloth, or greasy glass.

Now hear what blessings temperance can bring:
(Thus said our friend, and what he said I sing)
First health: the stomach cramm'd from ev'ry dish,
A tomb of boil'd and roast, and flesh and fish,   70
Where bile, and wind, and phlegm, and acid jar,
And all the man is one intestine war,
Remembers oft the school-boy's simple fare,
The temp'rate sleeps, and spirits light as air.

How pale, each worshipful and rev'rend guest
Rise from a clergy, or a city feast!
What life in all that ample body, say?
What heav'nly particle inspires the clay?
The soul subsides, and wickedly inclines
To seem but mortal, ev'n in sound divines.   80

On morning wings how active springs the mind
That leaves the load of yesterday behind?
How easy ev'ry labour it pursues?
How coming to the poet ev'ry muse?

Not but we may exceed, some holy time,
Or tir'd in search of truth, or search of rhyme;
Ill health some just indulgence may engage;
And more the sickness of long life, old age;
For fainting age what cordial drop remains,
If our intemp'rate youth the vessel drains?   90
    Our fathers prais'd rank ven'son. You suppose,
Perhaps, young men! our fathers had no nose.
Not so: a buck was then a week's repast,
And 'twas their point, I ween, to make it last;
More pleas'd to keep it till their friends should come,
Than eat the sweetest by themselves at home.
Why had not I in those good times my birth,
Ere coxcomb-pyes or coxcombs were on earth?
    Unworthy he, the voice of Fame to hear,
That sweetest music to an honest ear;   100
For 'faith, Lord Fanny! you are in the wrong,
The world's good word is better than a song;
Who has not learn'd, fresh sturgeon and ham-pye
Are no rewards for want, and infamy!
When luxury has lick'd up all thy pelf,
Curs'd by thy neighbours, thy trustees, thyself,
To friends, to fortune, to mankind a shame,
Think how posterity will treat thy name;
And buy a rope, that future times may tell
Thou hast at least bestow'd one penny well.   110
    'Right,' cries his lordship, 'for a rogue in need
To have a taste is insolence indeed :
In me 'tis noble, suits my birth and state,
My wealth unwieldy, and my heap too great.'
Then, like the sun, let bounty spread her ray
And shine that superfluity away.

Oh impudence of wealth! with all thy store,
How dar'st thou let one worthy man be poor?
Shall half the new-built churches round thee fall?
Make keys, build bridges, or repair White-hall: 120
Or to thy country let that heap be lent,
As M * * o's was, but not at five per cent.

Who thinks that fortune cannot change her mind,
Prepares a dreadful jest for all mankind.
And who stands safest? tell me, is it he
That spreads and swells in puff'd prosperity,
Or blest with little, whose preventing care
In peace provides fit arms against a war?

Thus Bethel spoke, who always speaks his thought,
And always thinks the very thing he ought: 130
His equal mind I copy what I can,
And as I love, would imitate the man.
In South-sea days not happier, when surmis'd
The lord of thousands, than if now excis'd;
In forest planted by a father's hand,
Than in five acres now of rented land.
Content with little I can piddle here
On brocoli and mutton, round the year;
But ancient friends (tho' poor, or out of play)
That touch my bell, I cannot turn away.   140
'Tis true, no turbots dignify my boards,
But gudgeons, flounders, what my Thames affords:
To Hounslow-heath I point and Bansted-down,
Thence comes your mutton, and these chicks my own:
From yon old walnut-tree a show'r shall fall;
And grapes, long ling'ring on my only wall,
And figs from standard and espalier join;
The dev'l is in you if you cannot dine:

Then chearful healths (your mistress shall have place)
And, what's more rare, a poet shall say grace.   150
　　Fortune not much of humbling me can boast:
Tho' double tax'd, how little have I lost!
My life's amusements have been just the same,
Before, and after standing armies came.
My lands are sold, my father's house is gone;
I'll hire another's; is not that my own,
And yours, my friends? thro' whose free-op'ning gate
None comes too early, none departs too late;
For I, who hold sage Homer's rule the best,
Welcome the coming, speed the going guest.   160
'Pray heav'n it last! (cries Swift!) as you go on;
I wish to God this house had been your own:
Pity! to build, without a son or wife;
Why, you'll enjoy it only all your life.'
Well, if the use be mine, can it concern one,
Whether the name belong to Pope or Vernon?
What's property? dear Swift! you see it alter
From you to me, from me to Peter Walter;
Or, in a mortgage, prove a lawyer's share;
Or, in a jointure, vanish from the heir;   170
Or in pure equity (the case not clear)
The Chanc'ry takes your rents for twenty year:
At best, it falls to some ungracious son,
Who cries, 'My father's damn'd, and all's my own.'
Shades, that to Bacon could retreat afford,
Become the portion of a booby lord;
And Helmsley, once proud Buckingham's delight,
Slides to a scriv'ner or a city knight.
Let lands and houses have what lords they will,
Let us be fix'd, and our own masters still.   180

SATIRES AND EPISTLES.

III.

To Lord Bolingbroke.

(HORACE, I EP. I.)

T. JOHN, whose love indulg'd my labours past,
Matures my present, and shall bound my last!
Why will you break the sabbath of my days?
Now sick alike of envy and of praise.
Public too long, ah let me hide my age!
See modest Cibber now has left the stage:
Our gen'rals now, retir'd to their estates,
Hang their old trophies o'er the garden-gates,
In life's cool ev'ning satiate of applause,
Nor fond of bleeding, ev'n in Brunswick's cause. 10
A voice there is, that whispers in my ear,
('Tis reason's voice, which sometimes one can hear)
'Friend Pope! be prudent, let your muse take
      breath,
And never gallop Pegasus to death;
Lest stiff, and stately, void of fire or force,
You limp, like Blackmore on a Lord Mayor's
      horse.'
   Farewell then verse, and love, and ev'ry toy,
The rhymes and rattles of the man or boy;

E

What right, what true, what fit we justly call,
Let this be all my care—for this is all: 20
To lay this harvest up, and hoard with haste,
What ev'ry day will want, and most, the last.
    But ask not, to what doctors I apply.
Sworn to no master, of no sect am I:
As drives the storm, at any door I knock:
And house with Montagne now, or now with Locke.
Sometimes a patriot, active in debate,
Mix with the world, and battle for the state,
Free as young Lyttelton, her cause pursue,
Still true to virtue, and as warm as true: 30
Sometimes with Aristippus, or St. Paul,
Indulge my candor, and grow all to all;
Back to my native moderation slide,
And win my way by yielding to the tide.
    Long, as to him who works for debt, the day,
Long as the night to her whose love's away,
Long as the year's dull circle seems to run,
When the brisk minor pants for twenty-one:
So slow th' unprofitable moments roll,
That lock up all the functions of my soul;   40
That keep me from myself; and still delay
Life's instant business to a future day:
That task, which as we follow, or despise,
The eldest is a fool, the youngest wise:
Which done, the poorest can no wants endure;
And which not done, the richest must be poor.
    Late as it is, I put myself to school,
And feel some comfort, not to be a fool.
Weak tho' I am of limb, and short of sight,
Far from a lynx, and not a giant quite;   50

I'll do what Mead and Cheselden advise,
To keep these limbs, and to preserve these eyes.
Not to go back, is somewhat to advance,
And men must walk at least before they dance.

　Say, does thy blood rebel, thy bosom move
With wretched av'rice, or as wretched love?
Know, there are words and spells, which can controll,
Between the fits, this fever of the soul;
Know, there are rhymes, which fresh and fresh apply'd
Will cure the arrant'st puppy of his pride.　　　60
Be furious, envious, slothful, mad, or drunk,
Slave to a wife, or vassal to a punk,
A Switz, a High-dutch, or a Low-dutch bear;
All that we ask is but a patient ear.

　'Tis the first virtue, vices to abhor;
And the first wisdom, to be fool no more.
But to the world no bugbear is so great,
As want of figure, and a small estate.
To either India see the merchant fly,
Scar'd at the spectre of pale poverty!　　　70
See him, with pains of body, pangs of soul,
Burn through the tropic, freeze beneath the pole!
Wilt thou do nothing for a nobler end,
Nothing, to make philosophy thy friend?
To stop thy foolish views, thy long desires,
And ease thy heart of all that it admires?
Here, wisdom calls: 'Seek virtue first, be bold!
As gold to silver, virtue is to gold.'
There, London's voice, 'Get money, money still!
And then let virtue follow, if she will.'　　　80
This, this the saving doctrine, preach'd to all,
From low St. James's up to high St. Paul;

From him whose quills stand quiver'd at his ear,
To him who notches sticks at Westminster.
    Barnard in spirit, sense, and truth abounds;
'Pray then, what wants he?' Fourscore thousand
      pounds;
A pension, or such harness for a slave
As Bug now has, and Dorimant would have.
Barnard, thou art a Cit, with all thy worth!
But Bug and D*l, their honours, and so forth.   90
    Yet ev'ry child another song will sing,
'Virtue, brave boys! 'tis virtue makes a king.'
True, conscious honour is to feel no sin,
He's armed without that's innocent within;
Be this thy screen, and this thy wall of brass;
Compar'd to this a minister's an ass.
    And say, to which shall our applause belong,
This new court-jargon, or the good old song?
The modern language of corrupted peers,
Or what was spoke at Cressy and Poitiers?   100
Who counsels best? who whispers, 'Be but great,
With praise or infamy leave that to fate;
Get place and wealth, if possible, with grace;
If not, by any means get wealth and place.'
For what? to have a box where eunuchs sing,
And foremost in the circle eye a king.
Or he, who bids thee face with steady view
Proud fortune, and look shallow greatness thro':
And, while he bids thee, sets th' example too?
If such a doctrine, in St. James's air,   110
Shou'd chance to make the well-drest rabble stare;
If honest S*z take scandal at a spark,
That less admires the palace than the park:

Faith I shall give the answer Reynard gave:
'I cannot like, dread Sir, your Royal Cave:
Because I see, by all the tracks about,
Full many a beast goes in, but none come out.'
Adieu to virtue, if you're once a slave:
Send her to court, you send her to her grave.

Well, if a king's a lion, at the least   120
The people are a many-headed beast:
Can they direct what measures to pursue,
Who know themselves so little what to do?
Alike in nothing but one lust of gold,
Just half the land would buy, and half be sold:
Their country's wealth our mightier misers drain,
Or cross, to plunder provinces, the main;
The rest, some farm the poor-box, some the pews;
Some keep assemblies, and would keep the stews;
Some with fat bucks on childless dotards fawn;   130
Some win rich widows by their chine and brawn;
While with the silent growth of ten per cent,
In dirt and darkness, hundreds stink content.

Of all these ways, if each pursues his own,
Satire, be kind, and let the wretch alone:
But shew me one who has it in his pow'r
To act consistent with himself an hour.
Sir Job sail'd forth, the ev'ning bright and still,
'No place on earth (he cry'd) like Greenwich hill!'
Up starts a palace, lo, th' obedient base   140
Slopes at its foot, the woods its sides embrace,
The silver Thames reflects its marble face.
Now let some whimsy, or that dev'l within
Which guides all those who know not what they mean,
But give the knight (or give his lady) spleen;

'Away, away! take all your scaffolds down,
For snug's the word : My dear! we'll live in town.
    At am'rous Flavio is the stocking thrown?
That very night he longs to lie alone.
The fool, whose wife elopes some thrice a quarter, 150
For matrimonial solace dies a martyr.
Did ever Proteus, Merlin, any witch,
Transform themselves so strangely as the rich?
Well, but the poor—The poor have the same itch;
They change their weekly barber, weekly news,
Prefer a new japanner to their shoes,
Discharge their garrets, move their beds, and run
(They know not whither) in a chaise and one;
They hire their sculler, and when once aboard,
Grow sick, and damn the climate—like a lord.   160
    You laugh, half beau half sloven if I stand,
My wig all powder, and all snuff my band;
You laugh, if coat and breeches strangely vary,
White gloves, and linen worthy Lady Mary!
But when no prelate's lawn with hair-shirt lin'd,
Is half so incoherent as my mind,
When, each opinion with the next at strife,
One ebb and flow of follies all my life,
I plant, root up; I build, and then confound;
Turn round to square, and square again to round; 170
You never change one muscle of your face,
You think this madness but a common case,
Nor once to Chanc'ry, nor to Hale apply;
Yet hang your lip, to see a seam awry!
Careless how ill I with myself agree,
Kind to my dress, my figure, not to me.
Is this my guide, philosopher, and friend?
This he, who loves me, and who ought to mend;

Who ought to make me (what he can, or none)
That man divine whom wisdom calls her own; 180
Great without title, without fortune bless'd;
Rich ev'n when plunder'd, honour'd while oppress'd;
Lov'd without youth, and follow'd without pow'r;
At home, tho' exil'd; free, tho' in the Tower;
In short, that reas'ning, high, immortal thing,
Just less than Jove, and much above a king;
Nay, half in heav'n, except (what's mighty odd)
A fit of vapours clouds this demy-god?

SATIRES AND EPISTLES.

IV.

To Mr. Murray.

OT to admire, is all the art I know,
   To make men happy, and to keep them so.'
Plain truth, dear Murray, needs no flow'rs of
   speech,
So take it in the very words of Creech.
   This vault of air, this congregated ball,
Self-center'd sun, and stars that rise and fall,
There are, my friend! whose philosophic eyes
Look thro', and trust the ruler with his skies,
To him commit the hour, the day, the year,
And view this dreadful All without a fear.   10
Admire we then what earth's low entrails hold,
Arabian shores, or Indian seas infold;
All the mad trade of fools and slaves for gold?
Or popularity? or stars and strings?
The mob's applauses, or the gifts of kings?
Say with what eyes we ought at courts to gaze,
And pay the great our homage of amaze?
   If weak the pleasure that from these can spring,
The fear to want them is as weak a thing:
Whether we dread, or whether we desire,   20
In either case. believe me, we admire;

Whether we joy or grieve, the same the curse,
Surpriz'd at better, or surpriz'd at worse.
Thus good or bad to one extreme betray
Th' unbalanc'd mind, and snatch the man away;
For virtue's self may too much zeal be had;
The worst of madmen is a saint run mad.
Go then, and if you can, admire the state
Of beaming diamonds, and reflected plate;
Procure a taste to double the surprize,   30
And gaze on Parian charms with learned eyes:
Be struck with bright brocade, or Tyrian dye,
Our Birth-day nobles' splendid livery.
If not so pleas'd, at council-board rejoice,
To see their judgments hang upon thy voice;
From morn to night, at senate, Rolls, and Hall,
Plead much, read more, dine late, or not at all.
But wherefore all this labour, all this strife?
For fame, for riches, for a noble wife?
Shall one whom nature, learning, birth conspir'd   40
To form, not to admire but be admir'd,
Sigh, while his Chloe blind to wit and worth
Weds the rich dulness of some son of earth?
Yet time ennobles, or degrades each line;
It brighten'd Craggs's, and may darken thine:
And what is fame? the meanest have their day,
The greatest can but blaze, and pass away.
Grac'd as thou art with all the pow'r of words,
So known, so honour'd, at the house of Lords:
Conspicuous scene! another yet is nigh,   50
(More silent far) where kings and poets lie;
Where Murray (long enough his country's pride)
Shall be no more than Tully, or than Hyde!

Rack'd with sciatics, martyr'd with the stone,
Will any mortal let himself alone?
See Ward by batter'd beaus invited over,
And desp'rate misery lays hold on Dover.
The case is easier in the mind's disease;
There all men may be cur'd whene'er they please.
Would ye be blest? despise low joys, low gains;   60
Disdain whatever Cornbury disdains;
Be virtuous, and be happy for your pains.
  But art thou one, whom new opinions sway,
One who believes as Tindal leads the way,
Who virtue and a Church alike disowns,
Thinks that but words, and this but brick and stones?
Fly then, on all the wings of wild desire,
Admire whate'er the maddest can admire:
Is wealth thy passion? Hence! from pole to pole,
Where winds can carry, or where waves can roll,   70
For Indian spices, for Peruvian gold,
Prevent the greedy, and out-bid the bold:
Advance thy golden mountain to the skies;
On the broad base of fifty thousand rise,
Add one round hundred, and (if that's not fair)
Add fifty more, and bring it to a square.
For, mark th' advantage; just so many score
Will gain a wife with half as many more,
Procure her beauty, make that beauty chaste,
And then such friends—as cannot fail to last.   80
A man of wealth is dubb'd a man of worth,
Venus shall give him form, and Anstis birth.
Believe me, many a German prince is worse,
Who proud of pedigree, is poor of purse.
His wealth brave Timon gloriously confounds;
Ask'd for a groat, he gives a hundred pounds;

Or if three ladies like a luckless play,
Takes the whole house upon the poet's day.
Now, in such exigencies not to need,
Upon my word, you must be rich indeed;   90
A noble superfluity it craves,
Not for yourself, but for your fools and knaves;
Something, which for your honour they may cheat,
And which it much becomes you to forget.
If wealth alone then make and keep us blest,
Still, still be getting, never, never rest.

But if to pow'r and place your passion lie,
If in the pomp of life consist the joy;
Then hire a slave, or (if you will) a lord
To do the honours, and to give the word;   100
Tell at your levee, as the crouds approach,
To whom to nod, whom take into your coach,
Whom honour with your hand: to make remarks,
Who rules in Cornwall, or who rules in Berks:
'This may be troublesome, is near the chair:
That makes three members, this can chuse a may'r.'
Instructed thus, you bow, embrace, protest,
Adopt him son, or cousin at the least,
Then turn about, and laugh at your own jest.

Or if your life be one continu'd treat,   110
If to live well means nothing but to eat;
Up, up! cries gluttony, 'tis break of day,
Go drive the deer, and drag the finny prey;
With hounds and horns go hunt an appetite;
So Russel did, but could not eat at night,
Call'd happy dog! the beggar at his door,
And envy'd thirst and hunger to the poor.

Or shall we ev'ry decency confound,
Thro' taverns, stews, and bagnio's take our round,

Go dine with Chartres, in each vice out-do   120
K * * l's lew'd cargo, or Ty * * y's crew,
From Latian syrens, French Circæan feasts,
Return'd well travell'd, and transformed to beasts,
Or for a titled punk, or foreign flame, ·
Renounce our country, and degrade our name?
   If, after all, we must with Wilmot own,
The cordial drop of life is love alone,
And Swift cry wisely, 'Vive la bagatelle!'
The man that loves and laughs, must sure do well.
Adieu; if this advice appear the worst,   130
E'en take the counsel which I gave you first;
Or better precepts if you can impart,
Why do, I'll follow them with all my heart.

SATIRES AND EPISTLES.

V.

To Augustus.

(Horace, 2 Epist. I.)

ADVERTISEMENT.

The reflections of Horace, and the judgments past in his Epistle to Augustus, seem'd so seasonable to the present times, that I could not help applying them to the use of my own country. The author thought them considerable enough to address them to his prince; whom he paints with the great and good qualities of a monarch, upon whom the Romans depended for the encrease of an absolute empire. But to make the poem entirely English, I was willing to add one or two of those which contribute to the happiness of a free people, and are more consistent with the welfare of our neighbours.

This Epistle will shew the learned world to have fallen into two mistakes: one, that Augustus was a patron of poets in general; whereas he not only prohibited all but the best writers to name him, but recommended that care even to the civil magistrate: Admonebat praetores, ne paterentur nomen suum obsolefieri, &c. The other, that this piece was only a general discourse of poetry; whereas it was an apology for the poets, in order to render Augustus more their patron. Horace here pleads the cause of his cotemporaries, first against the taste of the town, whose humour it was to magnify the authors of the preceding age; secondly against the court and nobility, who encouraged only the writers for the theatre; and lastly against the Emperor himself, who had conceived them of little use to the Government. He shews (by a view of the progress of learning, and the change of taste among the Romans) that the introduction of the polite arts of Greece had given the writers of his time great advantages over their predecessors; that their morals were much improved, and the licence of those ancient poets restrained: that

satire and comedy were become more just and useful; that whatever extravagances were left on the stage, were owing to the ill taste of
the nobility; that poets, under due regulations, were in many respects
useful to the State, and concludes, that it was upon them the Emperor
himelf must depend, for his fame with posterity.

We may farther learn from this Epistle, that Horace made his court to this
great prince by writing with a decent freedom toward him, with a just
contempt of his low flatterers, and with a manly regard to his own
character.

WHILE you, great patron of mankind! sustain
The balanc'd world, and open all the main;
Your country, chief, in arms abroad defend,
At home, with morals, arts, and laws amend;
How shall the muse, from such a monarch, steal
An hour, and not defraud the public weal?

 Edward and Henry, now the boast of fame,
And virtuous Alfred, a more sacred name,
After a life of gen'rous toils endur'd,
The Gaul subdu'd, or property secur'd,   10
Ambition humbled, mighty cities storm'd,
Or laws establish'd, and the world reform'd;
Clos'd their long glories with a sigh, to find
Th' unwilling gratitude of base mankind!
All human virtue, to its latest breath,
Finds envy never conquer'd, but by death.
The great Alcides, ev'ry labour past,
Had still this monster to subdue at last.
Sure fate of all, beneath whose rising ray
Each star of meaner merit fades away!   20
Oppress'd we feel the beam directly beat,
Those suns of glory please not till they set.

 To thee, the world its present homage pays,
The harvest early, but mature the praise:

Great friend of liberty! in kings a name
Above all Greek, above all Roman fame:
Whose word is truth, as sacred and rever'd,
As heav'n's own oracles from altars heard.
Wonder of Kings! like whom, to mortal eyes
None e'er has risen, and none e'er shall rise.   30

  Just in one instance, be it yet confest
Your people, Sir, are partial in the rest:
Foes to all living worth except your own,
And advocates for folly dead and gone.
Authors, like coins, grow dear as they grow old;
It is the rust we value, not the gold.
Chaucer's worst ribaldry is learn'd by rote,
And beastly Skelton heads of houses quote:
One likes no language but the Faery Queen;
A Scot will fight for Christ's Kirk o' the Green;   40
And each true Briton is to Ben so civil,
He swears the muses met him at The devil.

  Tho' justly Greece her eldest sons admires,
Why shou'd not we be wiser than our sires?
In ev'ry public virtue we excel;
We build, we paint, we sing, we dance as well,
And learned Athens to our art must stoop,
Could she behold us tumbling thro' a hoop.

  If time improve our wit as well as wine,
Say at what age a poet grows divine?   50
Shall we, or shall we not, account him so,
Who dy'd, perhaps, an hundred years ago?
End all dispute; and fix the year precise
When British bards begin t' immortalize?

  ' Who lasts a century can have no flaw,
I hold that wit a classic, good in law.'

Suppose he wants a year, will you compound?
And shall we deem him ancient, right and sound,
Or damn to all eternity at once,
At ninety-nine, a modern and a dunce?   60
    'We shall not quarrel for a year or two;
By courtesy of England, he may do.'
    Then, by the rule that made the horse-tail bare,
I pluck out year by year, as hair by hair,
And melt down ancients like a heap of snow:
While you, to measure merits, look in Stowe,
And estimating authors by the year,
Bestow a garland only on a bier.
    Shakespear, whom you and ev'ry play-house bill
Style the divine, the matchless, what you will,   70
For gain, not glory, wing'd his roving flight,
And grew immortal in his own despight.
Ben, old and poor, as little seem'd to heed
The life to come in ev'ry poet's creed.
Who now reads Cowley? if he pleases yet,
His moral pleases, not his pointed wit;
Forgot his Epic, nay Pindaric Art,
But still I love the language of his heart.
    'Yet surely, surely, these were famous men!
What boy but hears the sayings of old Ben?   80
In all debates where critics bear a part,
Not one but nods, and talks of Johnson's art,
Of Shakespear's nature, and of Cowley's wit;
How Beaumont's judgment check'd what Fletcher writ;
How Shadwell hasty, Wycherly was slow;
But, for the passions, Southern sure and Rowe.
These, only these, support the crouded stage,
From eldest Heywood down to Cibber's age.'

All this may be; the people's voice is odd,
It is, and it is not, the voice of God.   90
To Gammer Gurton if it give the bays,
And yet deny the Careless Husband praise,
Or say our fathers never broke a rule;
Why then, I say, the public is a fool.
But let them own, that greater faults than we
They had, and greater virtues, I'll agree.
Spenser himself affects the obsolete,
And Sydney's verse halts ill on Roman feet:
Milton's strong pinion now not heav'n can bound,
Now serpent-like in prose he sweeps the ground,   100
In quibbles angel and archangel join,
And God the Father turns a school-divine.
Not that I'd lop the beauties from his book,
Like slashing Bentley with his desp'rate hook,
Or damn all Shakespear, like th' affected fool
At court, who hates whate'er he read at school.
  But for the wits of either Charles's days,
The mob of gentlemen who wrote with ease ;
Sprat, Carew, Sedley, and a hundred more,
(Like twinkling stars the miscellanies o'er)   110
One simile, that solitary shines
In the dry desert of a thousand lines,
Or lengthen'd thought that gleams through many a page,
Has sanctify'd whole poems for an age.
I lose my patience, and I own it too,
When works are censur'd, not as bad but new ;
While if our elders break all reason's laws,
These fools demand not pardon, but applause.
  On Avon's bank, where flow'rs eternal blow,
If I but ask, if any weed can grow;   120

F

One tragic sentence if I dare deride,
Which Betterton's grave action dignify'd,
Or well-mouth'd Booth with emphasis proclaims,
(Tho' but, perhaps, a muster-roll of names)
How will our fathers rise up in a rage,
And swear, all shame is lost in George's age!
You'd think no fools disgrac'd the former reign,
Did not some grave examples yet remain,
Who scorn a lad should teach his father skill,
And, having once been wrong, will be so still.   130
He, who to seem more deep than you or I,
Extols old bards, or Merlin's prophecy,
Mistake him not; he envies, not admires,
And to debase the sons, exalts the sires.
Had ancient times conspir'd to disallow
What then was new, what had been ancient now?
Or what remain'd, so worthy to be read
By learned critics, of the mighty dead?

    In days of ease, when now the weary sword
Was sheath'd, and luxury with Charles restor'd;   140
In ev'ry taste of foreign courts improv'd,
'All, by the king's example, liv'd and lov'd.'
Then peers grew proud in horsemanship t' excell,
Newmarket's glory rose, as Britain's fell;
The soldier breath'd the gallantries of France,
And ev'ry flow'ry courtier writ romance.
Then marble, soften'd into life, grew warm,
And yielding metal flow'd to human form:
Lely on animated canvas stole
The sleepy eye, that spoke the melting soul.   150
No wonder then, when all was love and sport,
The willing muses were debauch'd at court:

On each enervate string they taught the note
To pant, or tremble thro' an eunuch's throat.

    But Britain, changeful as a child at play,
Now calls in princes, and now turns away.
Now Whig, now Tory, what we lov'd we hate;
Now all for pleasure, now for Church and State;
Now for prerogative, and now for laws;
Effects unhappy! from a noble cause.   160

    Time was, a sober Englishman wou'd knock
His servants up, and rise by five o'clock,
Instruct his family in ev'ry rule,
And send his wife to church, his son to school.
To worship like his fathers was his care;
To teach their frugal virtues to his heir;
To prove, that luxury could never hold;
And place, on good security, his gold.
Now times are chang'd, and one poetic itch
Has seiz'd the court and city, poor and rich: 170
Sons, sires, and grandsires, all will wear the bays,
Our wives read Milton, and our daughters plays,
To theatres, and to rehearsals throng,
And all our grace at table is a song.
I, who so oft renounce the muses, lye,
Not * * 's self e'er tells more fibs than I;
When sick of muse, our follies we deplore,
And promise our best friends to rhyme no more;
We wake next morning in a raging fit,
And call for pen and ink to show our wit.   180

    He serv'd a 'prenticeship, who sets up shop;
Ward try'd on puppies, and the poor, his drop;
Ev'n Radcliff's doctors travel first to France,
Nor dare to practise till they've learned to dance.

Who builds a bridge that never drove a pile?
(Should Ripley venture, all the world would smile)
But those who cannot write, and those who can,
All rhyme, and scrawl, and scribble, to a man.
    Yet, sir, reflect, the mischief is not great;
These madmen never hurt the Church or State :   190
Sometimes the folly benefits mankind ;
And rarely av'rice taints the tuneful mind.
Allow him but his plaything of a pen,
He ne'er rebels, or plots, like other men :
Flight of cashiers, or mobs, he'll never mind ;
And knows no losses while the muse is kind.
To cheat a friend, or ward, he leaves to Peter ;
The good man heaps up nothing but mere metre,
Enjoys his garden and his book in quiet ;
And then—a perfect hermit in his diet.   200
    Of little use the man you may suppose,
Who says in verse what others say in prose ;
Yet let me show, a poet's of some weight,
And, tho' no soldier, useful to the State.
What will a child learn sooner than a song?
What better teach a foreigner the tongue ?
What's long or short, each accent where to place,
And speak in public with some sort of grace.
I scarce can think him such a worthless thing,
Unless he praise some monster of a king ;   210
Or virtue, or religion turn to sport,
To please a lewd, or unbelieving court.
Unhappy Dryden ! In all Charles's days,
Roscommon only boasts unspotted bays ;
And in our own (excuse some courtly stains,
No whiter page than Addison remains.

He, from the taste obscene reclaims our youth,
And sets the passions on the side of truth,
Forms the soft bosom with the gentlest art,
And pours each human virtue in the heart.   220
Let Ireland tell, how wit upheld her cause,
Her trade supported, and supplied her laws;
And leave on Swift this grateful verse ingrav'd,
' The rights a court attack'd, a poet sav'd.'
Behold the hand that wrought a nation's cure,
Stretch'd to relieve the idiot and the poor,
Proud vice to brand, or injur'd worth adorn,
And stretch the ray to ages yet unborn.
Not but there are, who merit other palms;
Hopkins and Sternhold glad the heart with psalms: 230
The boys and girls whom charity maintains,
Implore your help in these pathetic strains:
How could devotion touch the country pews,
Unless the gods bestow'd a proper muse?
Verse chears their leisure, verse assists their work,
Verse prays for peace, or sings down Pope and Turk.
The silenc'd preacher yields to potent strain,
And feels that grace his pray'r besought in vain;
The blessing thrills thro' all the lab'ring throng,
And heav'n is won by violence of song.   240
　　Our rural ancestors, with little blest,
Patient of labour when the end was rest,
Indulg'd the day that hous'd their annual grain,
With feasts, and off'rings, and a thankful strain:
The joy their wives, their sons, and servants share,
Ease of their toil, and part'ners of their care:
The laugh, the jest, attendants on the bowl,
Smooth'd ev'ry brow and open'd ev'ry soul:

With growing years the pleasing licence grew,
And taunts alternate innocently flew.   250
But times corrupt, and nature ill-inclin'd,
Produc'd the point that left a sting behind;
Till friend with friend, and families at strife,
Triumphant malice rag'd thro' private life.
Who felt the wrong, or fear'd it, took th' alarm,
Appeal'd to law, and justice lent her arm.
At length, by wholesome dread of statutes bound,
The poets learn'd to please, and not to wound:
Most warp'd to flatt'ry's side; but some, more nice,
Preserv'd the freedom, and forbore the vice.   260
Hence satire rose, that just the medium hit,
And heals with morals what it hurts with wit.

We conquer'd France, but felt our captive's charms;
Her arts victorious triumph'd o'er our arms;
Britain to soft refinements less a foe,
Wit grew polite, and numbers learn'd to flow.
Waller was smooth; but Dryden taught to join
The varying verse, the full-resounding line,
The long majestic march, and energy divine.
Tho' still some traces of our rustic vein   270
And splay-foot verse remain'd, and will remain.
Late, very late, correctness grew our care,
When the tir'd nation breath'd from civil war.
Exact Racine, and Corneille's noble fire,
Show'd us that France had something to admire.
Not but the tragic spirit was our own,
And full in Shakespear, fair in Otway shone:
But Otway fail'd to polish or refine,
And fluent Shakespear scarce effac'd a line.
Ev'n copious Dryden wanted, or forgot,   280
The last and greatest art, the art to blot.

Some doubt, if equal pains, or equal fire
The humbler muse of comedy require.
But in known images of life, I guess
The labour greater, as th' indulgence less.
Observe how seldom ev'n the best succeed:
Tell me if Congreve's fools are fools indeed?
What pert, low dialogue has Farqu'ar writ!
How Van wants grace, who never wanted wit!
The stage how loosely does Astræa tread,   290
Who fairly puts all characters to bed!
And idle Cibber, how he breaks the laws,
To make poor Pinky eat with vast applause!
But fill their purse, our poets' work is done,
Alike to them, by pathos or by pun.

O you! whom vanity's light bark conveys
On fame's mad voyage by the wind of praise,
With what a shifting gale your course you ply,
For ever sunk too low, or borne too high!
Who pants for glory finds but short repose,   300
A breath revives him, or a breath o'erthrows.
Farewell the stage! if just as thrives the play,
The silly bard grows fat, or falls away.

There still remains, to mortify a wit,
The many-headed monster of the pit:
A senseless, worthless, and unhonour'd croud;
Who, to disturb their betters mighty proud,
Clatt'ring their sticks before ten lines are spoke,
Call for the farce, the bear, or the black-joke.
What dear delight to Britons farce affords!   310
Ever the taste of mobs, but now of lords;
Taste, that eternal wanderer, which flies
From heads to ears, and now from ears to eyes!

The play stands still; damn action and discourse,
Back fly the scenes, and enter foot and horse;
Pageants on pageants, in long order drawn,
Peers, heralds, bishops, ermin, gold and lawn;
The champion too! and, to complete the jest,
Old Edward's armour beams on Cibber's breast.
With laughter sure Democritus had dy'd,   320
Had he beheld an audience gape so wide.
Let bear or elephant be e'er so white,
The people, sure, the people are the sight!
Ah luckless poet! stretch thy lungs and roar,
That bear or elephant shall heed thee more;
While all its throats the gallery extends,
And all the thunder of the pit ascends!
Loud as the wolves on Orcas' stormy steep,
Howl to the roarings of the northern deep,
Such is the shout, the long-applauding note,   330
At Quin's high plume, or Oldfield's petticoat;
Or when from court a birth-day suit bestow'd,
Sinks the lost actor in the tawdry load.
Booth enters—hark! the universal peal!
'But has he spoken?' Not a syllable.
What shook the stage, and made the people stare?
Cato's long wig, flow'r'd gown, and lacquer'd chair.

   Yet lest you think I railly more than teach,
Or praise malignly arts I cannot reach,
Let me for once presume t' instruct the times,   340
To know the poet from the man of rhymes:
'Tis he, who gives my breast a thousand pains,
Can make me feel each passion that he feigns;
Inrage, compose, with more than magic art,
With pity, and with terror, tear my heart;

And snatch me, o'er the earth, or thro' the air,
To Thebes, to Athens, when he will, and where.
  But not this part of the poetic state
Alone, deserves the favour of the great:
Think of those authors, sir, who would rely   350
More on a reader's sense, than gazer's eye.
Or who shall wander where the muses sing?
Who climb their mountain, or who taste their spring?
How shall we fill a library with wit,
When Merlin's Cave is half unfurnish'd yet?
  My liege! why writers little claim your thought,
I guess; and, with their leave, will tell the fault:
We poets are, upon a poet's word,
Of all mankind the creatures most absurd:
The season, when to come, and when to go,   360
To sing, or cease to sing, we never know;
And if we will recite nine hours in ten,
You lose your patience, just like other men.
Then too we hurt ourselves, when to defend
A single verse, we quarrel with a friend;
Repeat unask'd; lament, the wit's too fine
For vulgar eyes, and point out ev'ry line.
But most, when straining with too weak a wing,
We needs will write epistles to the king;
And from the moment we oblige the town,   370
Expect a place, or pension from the crown;
Or dubb'd historians by express command,
T' enroll your triumphs o'er the seas and land,
Be call'd to court to plan some work divine,
As once for Louis, Boileau and Racine.
  Yet think, great sir! (so many virtues shown)
Ah think, what poet best may make them known;

Or chuse at least some minister of grace,
Fit to bestow the laureat's weighty place.

 Charles, to late times to be transmitted fair, 380
Assign'd his figure to Bernini's care;
And great Nassau to Kneller's hand decreed
To fix him graceful on the bounding steed;
So well in paint and stone they judg'd of merit:
But kings in wit may want discerning spirit.
The hero William, and the martyr Charles,
One knighted Blackmore, and one pension'd Quarles;
Which made old Ben, and surly Dennis swear,
'No Lord's anointed, but a Russian bear.'

 Not with such majesty, such bold relief, 390
The forms august, of king, or conqu'ring chief,
E'er swell'd on marble; as in verse have shin'd,
In polish'd verse, the manners and the mind.
Oh! could I mount on the Mæonian wing,
Your arms, your actions, your repose to sing!
What seas you travers'd, and what fields you fought!
Your country's peace, how oft, how dearly bought!
How barb'rous rage subsided at your word,
And nations wonder'd while they dropp'd the sword!
How, when you nodded, o'er the land and deep, 400
Peace stole her wing, and wrapt the world in sleep;
'Till earth's extremes your mediation own,
And Asia's tyrants tremble at your throne—
But verse, alas! your majesty disdains;
And I'm not us'd to panegyric strains:
The zeal of fools offends at any time,
But most of all, the zeal of fools in rhyme.
Besides, a fate attends on all I write,
That when I aim at praise, they say I bite.

A vile encomium doubly ridicules: 410
There's nothing blackens like the ink of fools.
If true, a woful likeness; and if lyes,
'Praise undeserv'd is scandal in disguise:'
Well may he blush, who gives it, or receives;
And when I flatter, let my dirty leaves,
Like journals, odes, and such forgotten things
As Eusden, Philips, Settle, writ of kings,
Cloath spice, line trunks, or flutt'ring in a row,
Befringe the rails of Bedlam and Soho.

SATIRES AND EPISTLES.

VI.

(HORACE, 2 Epist. 2.)

DEAR Col'nel, Cobham's and your country's friend!
You love a verse, take such as I can send.
A Frenchman comes, presents you with his boy,
Bows and begins—'This lad, sir, is of Blois:
Observe his shape how clean! his locks how curl'd!
My only son, I'd have him see the world:
His French is pure: his voice too—you shall hear.
Sir, he's your slave, for twenty pound a year.
Mere wax as yet, you fashion him with ease,
Your barber, cook, upholst'rer, what you please:
A perfect genius at an op'ra-song—   11
To say too much, might do my honour wrong.
Take him with all his virtues, on my word;
His whole ambition was to serve a lord:
But, sir, to you with what would I not part?
Tho' faith, I fear, 'twill break his mother's heart.
Once, and but once, I caught him in a lye,
And then, unwhipp'd, he had the grace to cry:
The fault he has I fairly shall reveal,
Cou'd you o'erlook but that, it is, to steal.'   20
    If, after this, you took the graceless lad,
Cou'd you complain, my friend, he prov'd so bad?
Faith, in such case, if you should prosecute,
I think Sir Godfrey should decide the suit;

Who sent the thief that stole the cash, away,
And punish'd him that put it in his way.

 Consider then, and judge me in this light;
I told you when I went, I could not write;
You said the same; and are you discontent
With laws, to which you gave your own assent? 30
Nay worse, to ask for verse at such a time!
D'ye think me good for nothing but to rhime?

 In Anna's wars, a soldier poor and old
Had dearly earn'd a little purse of gold:
Tir'd with a tedious march, one luckless night,
He slept, poor dog! and lost it, to a doit.
This put the man in such a desp'rate mind,
Between revenge, and grief, and hunger join'd,
Against the foe, himself, and all mankind,
He leap'd the trenches, scal'd a castle-wall, 40
Tore down a standard, took the fort and all.
' Prodigious well;' his great commander cry'd,
Gave him much praise, and some reward beside.
Next pleas'd his Excellence a town to batter;
(Its name I know not, and it's no great matter)
' Go on, my friend, he cry'd, see yonder walls!
Advance and conquer! go where glory calls!
More honours, more rewards, attend the brave.'
Don't you remember what reply he gave?
' D'ye think me, noble gen'ral, such a sot? 50
Let him take castles who has ne'er a groat.'

 Bred up at home, full early I begun
To read in Greek the wrath of Peleus' son.
Besides, my father taught me from a lad,
The better art to know the good from bad:

And little sure imported to remove,
To hunt for truth in Maudlin's learned grove.
But knottier points we knew not half so well,
Depriv'd us soon of our paternal cell;
And certain laws, by suff'rers thought unjust,   60
Deny'd all posts of profit or of trust:
Hopes after hopes of pious papists fail'd,
While mighty William's thund'ring arm prevail'd.
For right hereditary tax'd and fin'd,
He stuck to poverty with peace of mind;
And me, the muses help'd to undergo it;
Convict a papist he, and I a poet.
But (thanks to Homer) since I live and thrive,
Indebted to no prince or peer alive,
Sure I should want the care of ten Monroes,   70
If I would scribble, rather than repose.

   Years foll'wing years, steal something ev'ry day,
At last they steal us from ourselves away;
In one our frolics, one amusements end,
In one a mistress drops, in one a friend:
This subtle thief of life, this paltry time,
What will it leave me, if it snatch my rhime?
If ev'ry wheel of that unweary'd mill,
That turn'd ten thousand verses, now stands still?

   But after all, what wou'd you have me do?   80
When out of twenty I can please not two;
When this heroics only deigns to praise,
Sharp satire that, and that Pindaric lays?
One likes the pheasant's wing, and one the leg;
The vulgar boil, the learned roast an egg.
Hard task! to hit the palate of such guests,
When Oldfield loves, what Dartineuf detests.

But grant I may relapse, for want of grace,
Again to rhime; can London be the place?
Who there his muse, or self, or soul attends, 90
In crouds, and courts, law, business, feasts, and friends?
My counsel sends to execute a deed:
A poet begs me I will hear him read:
In Palace-yard at nine you'll find me there—
At ten for certain, sir, in Bloomsb'ry square—
Before the Lords at twelve my cause comes on—
There's a rehearsal, sir, exact at one.—
'Oh but a wit can study in the streets,
And raise his mind above the mob he meets.'
Not quite so well however as one ought; 100
A hackney coach may chance to spoil a thought;
And then a nodding beam, or pig of lead,
God knows, may hurt the very ablest head.
Have you not seen, at Guildhall's narrow pass,
Two aldermen dispute it with an ass?
And peers give way, exalted as they are,

* * * * * * *

Go, lofty poet! and in such a croud,
Sing thy sonorous verse—but not aloud.
Alas! to grottos and to groves we run, 110
To ease and silence, ev'ry muse's son:
Blackmore himself, for any grand effort,
Would drink and doze at Tooting or Earl's-court.
How shall I rhime in this eternal roar?
How match the bards whom none e'er match'd before?
The man, who, stretch'd in Isis' calm retreat,
To books and study gives sev'n years compleat,
See! strow'd with learned dust, his night-cap on,
He walks, an object new beneath the sun!

The boys flock round him, and the people stare: 120
So stiff, so mute! some statue you would swear,
Stept from its pedestal to take the air!
And here, while town, and court, and city roars,
With mobs, and duns, and soldiers, at their doors;
Shall I, in London, act this idle part?
Composing songs, for fools to get by heart?
    The Temple late two brother serjeants saw,
Who deem'd each other oracles of law ;
With equal talents, these congenial souls,
One lull'd th' Exchequer, and one stunn'd the Rolls ;
Each had a gravity would make you split,   131
And shook his head at Murray, as a wit.
'Twas, 'Sir, your law'—and 'Sir, your eloquence,'
'Yours, Cowper's manner'—and 'yours, Talbot's sense.'
Thus we dispose of all poetic merit,
Yours Milton's genius, and mine Homer's spirit.
Call Tibbald Shakespear, and he'll swear 'the nine,
Dear Cibber ! never match'd one ode of thine.
Lord! how we strut thro' Merlin's Cave, to see
No poets there, but Stephen, you, and me.   140
Walk with respect behind, while we at ease
Weave laurel crowns, and take what names we
        please.
'My dear Tibullus !' if that will not do,
Let me be Horace, and be Ovid you:
Or, I'm content, allow me Dryden's strains,
And you shall rise up Otway for your pains.'
Much do I suffer, much, to keep in peace
This jealous, waspish, wrong-head, rhiming race ;
And much must flatter, if the whim should bite
To court applause by printing what I write: 150

But let the fit pass o'er, I'm wise enough
To stop my ears to their confounded stuff.

   In vain bad rhimers all mankind reject,
They treat themselves with most profound respect;
'Tis to small purpose that you hold your tongue,
Each prais'd within, is happy all day long:
But how severely with themselves proceed
The men, who write such verse as we can read?
Their own strict judges, not a word they spare,
That wants or force, or light, or weight, or care,   160
Howe'er unwillingly it quits its place,
Nay tho' at Court, perhaps, it may find grace:
Such they'll degrade; and sometimes, in its stead,
In downright charity revive the dead;
Mark where a bold expressive phrase appears,
Bright thro' the rubbish of some hundred years;
Command old words that long have slept, to wake,
Words, that wise Bacon, or brave Rawleigh spake;
Or bid the new be English, ages hence,
For use will father what's begot by sense,   170
Pour the full tide of eloquence along,
Serenely pure, and yet divinely strong,
Rich with the treasures of each foreign tongue;
Prune the luxuriant, the uncouth refine,
But show no mercy to an empty line:
Then polish all, with so much life and ease,
You think 'tis nature, and a knack to please:
'But ease in writing flows from art, not chance;
As those move easiest who have learn'd to dance.'

   If such the plague and pains to write by rule,   180
Better (say I) be pleas'd, and play the fool;

G

Call, if you will, bad rhiming a disease,
It gives men happiness, or leaves them ease.
There liv'd in primo Georgii, they record,
A worthy member, no small fool, a lord;
Who, tho' the House was up, delighted sate,
Heard, noted, answer'd, as in full debate:
In all but this, a man of sober life,
Fond of his friend, and civil to his wife;
Not quite a madman, tho' a pasty fell,   190
And much too wise to walk into a well.
Him, the damn'd doctors and his friends immur'd,
They bled, they cupp'd, they purg'd; in short, they cur'd:
Whereat the gentleman began to stare—
My friends! he cry'd, * * * take you for your care!
That from a patriot of distinguish'd note,
Have bled and purg'd me to a simple vote.
    Well, on the whole, plain prose must be my fate,
Wisdom (curse on it) will come soon or late.
There is a time when poets will grow dull: 200
I'll e'en leave verses to the boys at school:
To rules of poetry no more confin'd,
I'll learn to smooth and harmonize my mind,
Teach ev'ry thought within its bounds to roll,
And keep the equal measure of the soul.
    Soon as I enter at my country door,
My mind resumes the thread it dropt before;
Thoughts, which at Hyde-park-corner I forgot,
Meet and rejoin me, in the pensive grot.
There all alone, and compliments apart,   210
I ask these sober questions of my heart:
    If, when the more you drink, the more you crave,
You tell the doctor; when the more you have,

The more you want, why not with equal ease
Confess as well your folly, as disease?
The heart resolves this matter in a trice,
' Men only feel the smart, but not the vice.'
   When golden angels cease to cure the evil,
You give all royal witchcraft to the devil:
When servile chaplains cry, that birth and place   220
Indue a peer with honour, truth, and grace,
Look in that breast, most dirty D * * *! be fair,
Say, can you find out one such lodger there?
Yet still, not heeding what your heart can teach,
You go to church to hear these flatt'rers preach.
   Indeed, could wealth bestow or wit or merit,
A grain of courage, or a spark of spirit,
The wisest man might blush, I must agree,
If D * * * lov'd sixpence, more than he.
   If there be truth in law, and use can give   230
A property, that's yours on which you live.
Delightful Abs-court, if its fields afford
Their fruits to you, confesses you its lord:
All Worldly's hens, nay, partridge, sold to town,
His ven'son too, a guinea makes your own:
He bought at thousands, what with better wit
You purchase as you want, and bit by bit;
Now, or long since, what diff'rence will be found?
You pay a penny, and he paid a pound.
   Heathcote himself, and such large-acred men,   240
Lords of fat E'sham, or of Lincoln fen,
Buy ev'ry stick of wood that lends them heat,
Buy ev'ry pullet they afford to eat.
Yet these are wights, who fondly call their own
Half that the dev'l o'erlooks from Lincoln town.

The laws of God, as well as of the land,
Abhor a perpetuity should stand:
Estates have wings, and hang in fortune's pow'r
Loose on the point of ev'ry wav'ring hour,
Ready, by force, or of your own accord,   250
By sale, at least by death, to change their lord.
Man? and for ever? wretch! what wou'dst thou have?
Heir urges heir, like wave impelling wave.
All vast possessions (just the same the case
Whether you call them villa, park, or chace)
Alas, my Bathurst! what will they avail?
Join Cotswold hills to Saperton's fair dale,
Let rising granaries and temples here,
There mingled farms and pyramids appear,
Link towns to towns with avenues of oak,   260
Enclose whole downs in walls, 'tis all a joke!
Inexorable death shall level all,
And trees, and stones, and farms, and farmer fall.

    Gold, silver, iv'ry, vases, sculptur'd high,
Paint, marble, gems, and robes of Persian dye,
There are who have not; and thank heav'n there are,
Who, if they have not, think not worth their care.

    Talk what you will of taste, my friend, you'll find
Two of a face, as soon as of a mind.
Why, of two brothers, rich and restless one   270
Plows, burns, manures, and toils from sun to sun;
The other slights, for women, sports, and wines,
All Townshend's turnips, and all Grovenor's mines:
Why one like Bu * with pay and scorn content,
Bows and votes on, in Court and Parliament;
One, driv'n by strong benevolence of soul,
Shall fly, like Oglethorpe, from pole to pole:

Is known alone to that directing pow'r,
Who forms the genius in the natal hour;
That God of Nature, who, within us still,   280
Inclines our action, not constrains our will;
Various of temper, as of face or frame,
Each individual: His great end the same.

    Yes, sir, how small soever be my heap,
A part I will enjoy, as well as keep.
My heir may sigh, and think it want of grace
A man so poor would live without a place;
But sure no statute in his favour says,
How free, or frugal, I shall pass my days:
I, who at sometimes spend, at others spare,   290
Divided between carelessness and care.
'Tis one thing madly to disperse my store;
Another, not to heed to treasure more;
Glad, like a boy, to snatch the first good day,
And pleas'd, if sordid want be far away.

    What is't to me (a passenger God wot)
Whether my vessel be first-rate or not?
The ship itself may make a better figure,
But I that sail, am neither less nor bigger.
I neither strut with ev'ry fav'ring breath,   300
Nor strive with all the tempest in my teeth.
In pow'r, wit, figure, virtue, fortune, plac'd
Behind the foremost, and before the last.

    ' But why all this of av'rice? I have none.'
I wish you joy, sir, of a tyrant gone;
But does no other lord it at this hour,
As wild and mad? the avarice of pow'r?
Does neither rage inflame, nor fear appall?
Not the black fear of death, that saddens all?

With terrors round, can reason hold her throne,   310
Despise the known, nor tremble at th' unknown?
Survey both worlds, intrepid and entire,
In spight of witches, devils, dreams and fire?
Pleas'd to look forward, pleas'd to look behind,
And count each birth-day with a grateful mind?
Has life no sourness, drawn so near its end;
Can'st thou endure a foe, forgive a friend?
Has age but melted the rough parts away,
As winter-fruits grow mild e'er they decay?
Or will you think, my friend, your business done,   320
When, of a hundred thorns, you pull out one?
   Learn to live well, or fairly make your will;
You've play'd, and lov'd, and eat, and drank your fill:
Walk sober off; before a sprightlier age
Comes titt'ring on, and shoves you from the stage:
Leave such to trifle with more grace and ease,
Whom folly pleases, and whose follies please.

EPILOGUE TO THE SATIRES AND EPISTLES.

IN TWO DIALOGUES.

MDCCXXXVIII.

DIALOGUE I.

Fr NOT twice a twelve-month you appear in print,
And when it comes, the Court see nothing in't.
You grow correct, that once with rapture writ,
And are, besides, too moral for a wit.
Decay of parts, alas! we all must feel—
Why now, this moment, don't I see you steal?
'Tis all from Horace; Horace long before ye
Said, 'Tories call'd him Whig, and Whigs a
    Tory;'
And taught his Romans, in much better metre,
'To laugh at fools who put their trust in Peter.' 10
But Horace, sir, was delicate, was nice;
Bubo observes, he lash'd no sort of vice:
Horace would say, Sir Billy serv'd the Crown,
Blunt could do bus'ness, H*ggins knew the
    town;
In Sappho touch the failings of the sex,
In rev'rend bishops note some small neglects,
And own the Spaniard did a waggish thing,
Who cropt our ears, and sent them to the king.

His sly, polite, insinuating style
Could please at Court, and make Augustus smile: 20
An artful manager, that crept between
His friend and shame, and was a kind of screen.
But 'faith your very friends will soon be sore;
Patriots there are, who wish you'd jest no more—
And where's the glory? 'twill be only thought
The great man never offer'd you a groat.
Go see Sir Robert —— *P.* See Sir Robert!—hum—
And never laugh—for all my life to come?
Seen him I have, but in his happier hour
Of social pleasure, ill-exchang'd for pow'r;   30
Seen him, uncumber'd with the venal tribe,
Smile without art, and win without a bribe.
Would he oblige me? let me only find,
He does not think me what he thinks mankind.
Come, come, at all I laugh he laughs, no doubt;
The only diff'rence is, I dare laugh out.

   F. Why yes: with scripture still you may be free;
A horse-laugh, if you please, at honesty;
A joke on Jekyl, or some odd old Whig
Who never chang'd his principle, or wig: 40
A patriot is a fool in ev'ry age,
Whom all lord chamberlains allow the stage:
These nothing hurts; they keep their fashion still,
And wear their strange old virtue, as they will.

   If any ask you, 'Who's the man, so near
His prince, that writes in verse, and has his ear?'
Why, answer, Lyttelton, and I'll engage
The worthy youth shall ne'er be in a rage:
But were his verses vile, his whisper base,
You'd quickly find him in Lord Fanny's case.   50

Sejanus, Wolsey, hurt not honest Fleury,
But well may put some statesmen in a fury.
  Laugh then at any, but at fools or foes;
These you but anger, and you mend not those.
Laugh at your friends, and, if your friends are sore,
So much the better, you may laugh the more.
To vice and folly to confine the jest,
Sets half the world, God knows, against the rest;
Did not the sneer of more impartial men
At sense and virtue, balance all agen.   60
Judicious wits spread wide the ridicule,
And charitably comfort knave and fool.
  P. Dear sir, forgive the prejudice of youth:
Adieu distinction, satire, warmth, and truth!
Come, harmless characters that no one hit;
Come, Henley's oratory, Osborn's wit!
The honey dropping from Favonio's tongue,
The flow'rs of Bubo, and the flow of Y * * ng!
The gracious dew of pulpit eloquence,
And all the well-whipt cream of courtly sense,   70
That first was H * * vy's, F * * 's next, and then
The S * * te's, and then H * * vy's once agen.
O come, that easy, Ciceronian style,
So Latin, yet so English all the while,
As, tho' the pride of Middleton and Bland,
All boys may read, and girls may understand!
Then might I sing, without the least offence,
And all I sung should be the nation's sense;
Or teach the melancholy muse to mourn,
Hang the sad verse on Carolina's urn,   80
And hail her passage to the realms of rest,
All parts perform'd, and all her children blest!

So—satire is no more—I feel it die—
No Gazetteer more innocent than I—
And let, a God's-name, ev'ry fool and knave
Be grac'd thro' life, and flatter'd .in his grave.
   F. Why so? if satire knows its time and place,
You still may lash the greatest—in disgrace;
For merit will by turns forsake them all;
Would you know when? exactly when they fall.   90
But let all satire in all changes spare
Immortal S * * k, and grave De * * * re.
Silent and soft, as saints remove to heav'n,
All tyes dissolv'd, and ev'ry sin forgiv'n,
These may some gentle ministerial wing
Receive, and place for ever near a king!
There, where no passion, pride, or shame transport,
Lull'd with the sweet nepenthe of a court;
There, where no father's, brother's, friend's disgrace
Once break their rest, or stir them from their place:
But past the sense of human miseries,   101
All tears are wip'd for ever from all eyes;
No cheek is known to blush, no heart to throb,
Save when they lose a question, or a job.
   P. Good heav'n forbid, that I should blast their glory,
Who know how like Whig ministers to Tory,
And when three sov'reigns dy'd, could scarce be vext,
Consid'ring what a gracious prince was next.
Have I, in silent wonder, seen such things
As pride in slaves, and avarice in kings;   110
And at a peer, or peeress, shall I fret,
Who starves a sister, or forswears a debt?
Virtue, I grant you, is an empty boast;
But shall the dignity of vice be lost?

Ye gods! shall Cibber's son, without rebuke,
Swear like a lord, or Rich * * * *
A fav'rite's porter with his master vie,
Be brib'd as often, and as often lie?
Shall Ward draw contracts with a statesman's skill?
Or Japhet pocket, like his grace, a will?   120
Is it for Bond, or Peter, paltry things!
To pay their debts, or keep their faith, like kings?
If Blount dispatch'd himself, he play'd the man,
And so may'st thou, illustrious Passeran!
But shall a printer, weary of his life,
Learn, from their books, to hang himself and wife?
This, this, my friend, I cannot, must not bear;
Vice thus abus'd, demands a nation's care:
This calls the church to deprecate our sin,
And hurls the thunder of the laws on gin.   130
    Let modest Foster, if he will, excell
Ten metropolitans in preaching well;
A simple Quaker, or a Quaker's wife,
Out-do Landaffe in doctrine,—yea in life:
Let humble Allen, with an aukward shame,
Do good by stealth, and blush to find it fame.
Virtue may chuse the high or low degree,
'Tis just alike to virtue, and to me;
Dwell in a monk, or light upon a king,
She's still the same, belov'd, contented thing.   140
Vice is undone, if she forgets her birth,
And stoops from angels to the dregs of earth:
But 'tis the fall degrades her * * *
Let greatness own her, and she's mean no more,
Her birth, her beauty, crowds and courts confess,
Chaste matrons praise her, and grave bishops bless;

In golden chains the willing world she draws,
And hers the gospel is, and hers the laws,
Mounts the tribunal, lifts her scarlet head,
And sees pale virtue carted in her stead.   150
Lo! at the wheels of her triumphal car,
Old England's genius, rough with many a scar,
Dragg'd in the dust! his arms hang idly round,
His flag inverted trails along the ground!
Our youth, all liv'ry'd o'er with foreign gold,
Before her dance: behind her, crawl the old!
See thronging millions to the pagod run,
And offer country, parent, wife, or son!
Hear her black trumpet thro' the land proclaim,
That not to be corrupted is the shame.   160
In soldier, churchman, patriot, man in pow'r,
'Tis av'rice all, ambition is no more!
See, all our nobles begging to be slaves!
See, all our fools aspiring to be knaves!
The wit of cheats, the courage * * *
Are what ten thousand envy and adore:
All, all look up, with reverential awe,
At crimes that 'scape, or triumph o'er the law:
While truth, worth, wisdom, daily they decry—
'Nothing is sacred now but villainy.'   170
   Yet may this verse (if such a verse remain)
Show there was one who held it in disdain.

EPILOGUE TO THE SATIRES.

MDCCXXXVIII.

DIALOGUE II.

Fr. 'TIS all a libel—Paxton, sir, will say.
    P. Not yet, my friend! to morrow 'faith it may;
And for that very cause I print to day.
How should I fret to mangle ev'ry line,
In rev'rence to the sins of thirty-nine!
Vice with such giant strides comes on amain,
Invention strives to be before in vain;
Feign what I will, and paint it e'er so strong,
Some rising genius sins up to my song.
    F. Yet none but you by name the guilty
        lash;   10
Ev'n Guthry saves half Newgate by a dash.
Spare then the person, and expose the vice.
    P. How, sir! not damn the sharper, but
        the dice?
Come on then, satire! gen'ral, unconfin'd,
Spread thy broad wing, and souce on all the kind.
Ye statesmen, priests, of one religion all!
Ye tradesmen, vile, in army, court, or hall!
Ye rev'rend atheists. *F.* Scandal! name them,
        Who?
    P. Why that's the thing you bid me not
        to do.

Who starv'd a sister, who forswore a debt,   20
I never nam'd; the town's enquiring yet.
The pois'ning dame— *F.* You mean— *P.* I don't.—
        F. You do.
    P. See, now I keep the secret, and not you!
The bribing statesman—*F.* Hold, too high you go.
    P. The brib'd elector—*F.* There you stoop too low.
    P. I fain would please you, if I knew with what;
Tell me, which knave is lawful game, which not?
Must great offenders, once escap'd the crown,
Like royal harts, be never more run down?
Admit your law to spare the knight requires,   30
As beasts of nature may we hunt the squires?
Suppose I censure—you know what I mean—
To save a bishop, may I name a dean?
    F. A dean, sir? no: his fortune is not made,
You hurt a man that's rising in the trade.
    P. If not the tradesman who set up to day,
Much less the 'prentice who to morrow may.
Down, down, proud satire! tho' a realm be spoil'd,
Arraign no mightier thief than wretched Wild;
Or, if a court or country's made a job,   40
Go drench a pick-pocket, and join the mob.
    But, sir, I beg you, for the love of vice!
The matter's weighty, pray consider twice;
Have you less pity for the needy cheat,
The poor and friendless villain, than the great?
Alas! the small discredit of a bribe
Scarce hurts the lawyer, but undoes the scribe.
Then better sure it charity becomes
To tax directors, who, thank God, have plums;
Still better, ministers; or, if the thing   50
May pinch ev'n there—why lay it on a king.

F. Stop! stop!

       P. Must satire, then, nor rise nor fall?
Speak out, and bid me blame no rogues at all.

  F. Yes, strike that Wild, I'll justify the blow.

  P. Strike? why the man was hang'd ten years ago:
Who now that obsolete example fears?
Ev'n Peter trembles only for his ears.

  F. What always Peter? Peter thinks you mad,
You make men desp'rate, if they once are bad:
Else might he take to virtue some years hence—   60

  P. As S * * k, if he lives, will love the Prince.

  F. Strange spleen to S * * k!

            P. Do I wrong the man?
God knows, I praise a courtier where I can.
When I confess, there is who feels for fame,
And melts to goodness, need I Scarb'row name?
Pleas'd let me own, in Esher's peaceful grove,
Where Kent and nature vye for Pelham's love,
The scene, the master, opening to my view,
I sit and dream I see my Craggs anew!

  Ev'n in a bishop I can spy desert;   70
Secker is decent, Rundel has a heart,
Manners with candour are to Benson giv'n,
To Berkley, ev'ry virtue under heav'n.

  But does the court a worthy man remove?
That instant, I declare, he has my love:
I shun his zenith, court his mild decline;
Thus Somers once, and Halifax, were mine.
Oft, in the clear, still mirrour of retreat,
I study'd Shrewsbury, the wise and great:
Carleton's calm sense, and Stanhope's noble flame,   80
Compar'd, and knew their gen'rous end the same:

How pleasing Atterbury's softer hour!
How shin'd the soul, unconquer'd in the Tow'r!
How can I Pult'ney, Chesterfield forget,
While Roman spirit charms, and Attic wit:
Argyll, the state's whole thunder born to wield,
And shake alike the senate and the field:
Or Wyndham, just to freedom and the throne,
The master of our passions, and his own:
Names, which I long have lov'd, nor lov'd in vain,
Rank'd with their friends, not number'd with their
   train;   91
And if yet higher the proud list should end,
Still let me say! No follower, but a friend.
 Yet think not, friendship only prompts my lays;
I follow virtue; where she shines, I praise:
Point she to priest or elder, Whig or Tory,
Or round a Quaker's beaver cast a glory.
I never, to my sorrow I declare,
Din'd with the Man of Ross, or my Lord May'r.
Some, in their choice of friends (nay, look not grave)
Have still a secret byass to a knave: 101
To find an honest man I beat about,
And love him, court him, praise him, in or out.
 F. Then why so few commended?
         P. Not so fierce;
Find you the virtue, and I'll find the verse.
But random praise—the task can ne'er be done;
Each mother asks it for her booby son,
Each widow asks it for 'the best of men,'
For him she weeps, for him she weds agen.
Praise cannot stoop, like satire, to the ground; 110
The number may be hang'd, but not be crown'd.

Enough for half the greatest of these days,
To 'scape my censure, not expect my praise.
Are they not rich? what more can they pretend?
Dare they to hope a poet for their friend?
What Richelieu wanted, Louis scarce could gain,
And what young Ammon wish'd, but wish'd in vain.
No pow'r the Muse's friendship can command;
No pow'r, when Virtue claims it, can withstand:
To Cato, Virgil pay'd one honest line;   120
O let my country's friends illumine mine!
—What are you thinking? *F.* Faith the thought's no sin,
I think your friends are out, and would be in.

  P. If merely to come in, Sir, they go out,
The way they take is strangely round about.

  F. They too may be corrupted, you'll allow?

  P. I only call those knaves who are so now.
Is that too little? Come then, I'll comply—
Spirit of Arnall! aid me while I lie.
Cobham's a coward, Polwarth is a slave,   130
And Lyttelton a dark, designing knave,
St. John has ever been a wealthy fool—
But let me add, Sir Robert's mighty dull,
Has never made a friend in private life,
And was, besides, a tyrant to his wife.

  But pray, when others praise him, do I blame?
Call Verres, Wolsey, any odious name?
Why rail they then, if but a wreath of mine,
Oh all-accomplish'd St. John! deck thy shrine?

  What? shall each spurgall'd hackney of the day, 140
When Paxton gives him double pots and pay,
Or each new-pension'd sycophant, pretend
To break my windows if I treat a friend;

Then wisely plead, to me they meant no hurt,
But 'twas my guest at whom they threw the dirt?
Sure, if I spare the minister, no rules
Of honour bind me, not to maul his tools;
Sure, if they cannot cut, it may be said
His saws are toothless, and his hatchets lead.

 It anger'd Turenne, once upon a day,   150
To see a footman kick'd that took his pay:
But when he heard th' affront the fellow gave,
Knew one a man of honour, one a knave,
The prudent gen'ral turn'd it to a jest,
And begg'd, he'd take the pains to kick the rest:
Which not at present having time to do—
F. Hold Sir! for God's sake, where's th' affront to you?
Against your worship when had S * * k writ?
Or P * ge pour'd forth the torrent of his wit?
Or grant the bard whose distich all commend 160
[In pow'r a servant, out of pow'r a friend]
To W * * le guilty of some venial sin;
What's that to you who ne'er was out nor in?

 The priest whose flattery be-dropt the crown,
How hurt he you? he only stain'd the gown.
And how did, pray, the florid youth offend,
Whose speech you took, and gave it to a friend?
P. Faith, it imports not much from whom it came;
Whoever borrow'd, could not be to blame,
Since the whole house did afterwards the same. 170
Let courtly wits to wits afford supply,
As hog to hog in huts of Westphaly;

  * * * * * * *

P. But hear me further—Japhet, 'tis agreed,
Writ not, and Chartres scarce could write or read,

In all the courts of Pindus guiltless quite;
But pens can forge, my friend, that cannot write;
And must no egg in Japhet's face be thrown,
Because the deed he forg'd was not my own?   190
Must never patriot then declaim at gin,
Unless, good man! he has been fairly in?
No zealous pastor blame a failing spouse,
Without a staring reason on his brows?
And each blasphemer quite escape the rod,
Because the insult's not on man, but God?

   Ask you what provocation I have had?
The strong antipathy of good to bad.
When truth or virtue an affront endures,
Th' affront is mine, my friend, and should be yours.
Mine, as a foe profess'd to false pretence,   201
Who think a coxcomb's honour like his sense;
Mine, as a friend to ev'ry worthy mind;
And mine as man, who feel for all mankind.

   F. You're strangely proud.

              P. So proud, I am no slave.
So impudent, I own myself no knave:
So odd, my country's ruin makes me grave.
Yes, I am proud; I must be proud, to see
Men not afraid of God, afraid of me:
Safe from the bar, the pulpit, and the throne,   210
Yet touch'd and sham'd by ridicule alone.

   O sacred weapon! left for truth's defence,
Sole dread of folly, vice, and insolence!
To all but heav'n directed hands deny'd,
The Muse may give thee, but the Gods must guide:
Rev'rent I touch thee! but with honest zeal;
To rouse the watchmen of the public weal,

To virtue's work provoke the tardy Hall,
And goad the prelate slumb'ring in his stall.
Ye tinsel insects! whom a court maintains,   220
That counts your beauties only by your stains,
Spin all your cobwebs o'er the eye of day!
The Muse's wing shall brush them all away:
All his Grace preaches, all his Lordship sings,
All that makes saints of queens, and gods of kings,
All, all but truth, drops dead-born from the press,
Like the last Gazette, or the last Address.

When black ambition stains a public cause,
A monarch's sword when mad vain-glory draws,
Not Waller's wreath can hide the nation's scar,   230
Not Boileau turn the feather to a star.

Not so, when diadem'd with rays divine,
Touch'd with the flame that breaks from virtue's shrine,
Her priestess Muse forbids the good to die,
And opes the temple of eternity.
There, other trophies deck the truly brave,
Than such as Anstis casts into the grave;
Far other stars than * and * * wear,
And may descend to Mordington from Stair;
Such as on Hough's unsully'd mitre shine,   240
Or beam, good Digby, from a heart like thine.
Let envy howl, while heav'n's whole chorus sings,
And bark at honour not confer'd by kings;
Let flatt'ry sick'ning see the incense rise,
Sweet to the world, and grateful to the skies:
Truth guards the poet, sanctifies the line,
And makes immortal, verse as mean as mine.

Yes, the last pen for freedom let me draw,
When truth stands trembling on the edge of law;

Here, last of Britons! let your names be read; 250
Are none, none living? let me praise the dead,
And for that cause which made your fathers shine,
Fall by the votes of their degen'rate line.

F. Alas! alas! pray end what you began,
And write next winter more Essays on Man.

NOTES.

PROLOGUE TO THE SATIRES AND EPISTLES.

1735.

An Epistle to Dr. Arbuthnot. In Warburton's ed. (1751) entitled, An Apology for Himself and his Writings.

John Arbuthnot, M.D., Fellow of the College of Physicians, and Physician in Ordinary to Queen Anne. He had wit, and not only literature, but even learning. His 'Tables of Ancient Coins, Weights, and Measures' (1727) was for a long time the standard work on the subject. He lived with the wits of the Tory party, and formed one of the Scriblerus Club (1714), of which Harley, Atterbury, Pope, Congreve, Gay, and Swift were members. At the date of this Epistle he had retired to Hampstead, 'so reduced by a dropsy and an asthma, that I could neither sleep, breathe, eat, or move.' Letter to Swift, Oct. 4, 1734. He died Feb. 27, 1735. The Epistle was published in January of that year. Cowper (Letters, March 21, 1784) says of Johnson's Poets: 'I know not but one might search these eight volumes with a candle to find a man, and not find one, unless, perhaps, Arbuthnot were he.'

The line of argument by which satire is defended in this Epistle is sketched in a letter actually written by Pope to Arbuthnot, July 26, 1734. It is a reply to a letter in which Arbuthnot exhorts the poet to continue to satirise vice and folly, 'but with a due regard to your own safety.'

Johnson, Life of Pope: 'The Epistle to Dr. Arbuthnot seems to be derived in its first design from Boileau's address "à son esprit," Satire 9. They are both an apology by the poet for satire.'

A remote resemblance may also be traced to Young's Two Epistles to Mr. Pope, concerning the Authors of the Age (1730).

l. 1. *good John.* Pope's Will, Carruthers' Life, p. 453: 'To my servant, John Searle, who has faithfully and ably served me many years, I give the sum of £100.' He is called 'the gardener' in the Plan of Mr. Pope's Garden, 1745. In 1735 he had been with Pope eleven years.

l 2. *Tye up the knocker.* Cf. Gay, Trivia, 2. 467 (1715):

> 'Where the brass-knocker, wrapt in flannel-band,
> Forbids the thunder of the footman's hand.'

l. 3. *dog-star.* Dunciad, 4. 9:

> 'Now flam'd the dogstar's unpropitious ray,
> Smote every brain, and wither'd every bay.'

In this Epistle the 'flagrantis atrox hora caniculæ' is represented as inflam‹ matory, not withering.

l. 6. *recite.* The 'recitator acerbus,' who insisted on making his friends listen to his verses, is a standing type of bore in the Latin literature of the first century A.D. Cf. Horat. A.P. 474:

> 'Indoctum doctumque fugat recitator acer¦us,
> Quem vero arripuit, tenet occiditque legendo,
> Non missura cutem nisi plena cruoris hirudo.'

The race was reproduced in France in the reign of Louis XIV., and is described by Boileau (L'Art Poét. c. 4):

> 'De ses vains écrits lecteur harmonieux
> Aborde en récitant quiconque le salue,
> Et poursuit de ses vers les passants dans la rue.'

l. 8. *They pierce my thickets, through my grot they glide.* The grounds of Pope's villa at Twickenham, altogether about five acres, were cut in two by the turnpike road leading from London to Hampton Court. To obviate the awkwardness of crossing this road, he had an underground passage constructed, at an expense of £1,000. It terminated in a kind of open temple, 'wholly composed of shells in the rustic manner.' Pope to Edward Blount. This was *my grot; my thicket*, is perhaps a shrubbery called 'The Grove' in the Plan of 1745, in which it is No. 12.

l. 13. *Mint.* Suffolk House in Southwark was converted into a mint for coinage. Being afterwards pulled down, on its site were built 'many small cottages, of great rents, to the increasing of beggars.' Stow, Survey, 2. 18. The whole district, containing several streets and alleys, was a sanctuary for debtors. Young, Ep. to Mr. Pope (1730):

> 'E'en George's praise is dated from the *Mint*.'

l. 14. *Happy ! to catch me just at dinner-time.* An unpardonable feature of Pope's satire is his constantly harping upon the beggary and miseries of poor authors. (See Introd. p. 14.) When we call to mind that he owed his own easy circumstances to the Homer subscription, we are reminded of his own line on Addison,

> 'And hate for arts that caus'd himself to rise.'

The same want of good feeling is chargeable on Boileau, who could find pleasure in satirising indigence; e.g. L'Art Poétique, c. 4:

'Et libre du souci qui trouble Colletet,
N'attend pas pour dîner le succès d'un sonnet.'

l. 15. *bemus'd.* Richardson (Dict.) quotes Fawkes, Horace, 1 Ep. 5 :

'Bemus'd in wine the bard his duns forgets,
And drinks serene oblivion to his debts.'

l. 16. *maudlin.* Wedgwood, Dict., 'given to crying, as the Magdalene is commonly represented. Hence, crying or sentimentally drunk, half-drunk.' More probably it is related to the Engl. *moider, moidering;* perhaps also connected with *muddle.*

l. 20.   *scrawls*
With desp'rate charcoal round his darken'd walls.

The scribbling poet in Boileau (L'Art Poét. c. 1) is made to 'charbonner de ses vers les murs d'un cabaret ;' a decorous imitation of Martial, 12. 61 :

'Carbone rudi putrique creta
Scribit carmina quæ legunt . . .'

Nathaniel Lee is probably glanced at ; see below, Sat. and Ep. 1. 100. Wither, when confined to the Tower in the reign of James I., wrote with ochre on his trencher verses which he afterwards printed. Pope's description was almost literally realised in the melancholy history of Christopher Smart, who, in 1763, being in confinement, indented a poem on the wainscot of his cell with the head of a key.

l. 23. *Arthur.* Arthur Moore, of whom Burnet says, Own Time, 2. 622, that 'he had risen from being a footman without any education, to be a great dealer in trade.' A full character of him is given in Speaker Onslow's note on the passage. Burnet, Own Time, Oxford ed., vol. vi. p. 162.

giddy son. James Moore Smythe, son of Arthur Moore. For notice of him, see Pope's note, Dunciad, 2. 50; and below, l. 385.

l. 27. *Friend to my life! which did not you prolong.* Cf. Young, Night Thoughts, Night 4 :

'Alive by miracle, or what is next,
Alive by Mead !'

l. 33. *Seiz'd and ty'd down to judge.* From Horace, 1 Sat. 3. 89 : 'porrecto jugulo captivus ut audit.' Horace's allusion is to the mythological story of Silenus, seized in the gardens of Midas. The earliest version of this favourite subject of Greek artists and poets is that of Theophrastus, 'Eudemos ;' ap. Plutarch, Consol. ad Apoll. 115 b.

l. 40. *nine years.* Hor. Ars Poet. 388, 'Nonum prematur in annum.'

l. 41. *high in Drury-lane.* Drury-lane and the Strand were the places where most of the gentry had lived before the Civil War. But after the Revolution fashion moved further west, Soho became the aristocratic quarter, and Drury-lane was left to poor authors and doubtful characters. Cf. Gay, Trivia :

'O, may thy virtue guard thee through the roads
　　Of Drury's mazy courts and dark abodes!'

l. 43. *prints before term ends*, i. e. before the end of the London season. Trinity Term ended three weeks, or thereabouts, after Trinity Sunday.

l. 46. *I'm all submission, what you'd have it, make it.* From Boileau, L'Art Poét. c. 1 :

'Vous avez sur ses vers un pouvoir despotique.
　　Mais tout ce beau discours dont il vient vous flatter,
　　N'est rien qu'un piége adroit pour vous les réciter.'

l. 49. *Pitholeon.* A name borrowed from Hor. 1 Sat. 10. 22.

l. 51. *but here's a letter.* Refers to Thomas Cooke, of whom Pope says (Dunciad, 2. 138, note), that he wrote against him in the 'British,' 'London,' and 'Daily' Journals, and at the same time wrote a letter to him protesting his innocence.

l. 61. *Fir'd that the house reject him, ' 'Sdeath I'll print it,
　　And shame the fools.'*

Taken by Horace and James Smith as the motto for their Rejected Addresses, 1813.

l. 62. *Lintot.* Bernard Lintot had ceased to publish for Pope some years before this. He had been disappointed in the expectations he had formed of the sale of the Odyssey, and this had led to a quarrel. Pope's celebrated ride to Oxford in company with Lintot took place twenty years before, in 1715, the year in which the first volume of the Iliad appeared.

l. 69. *Midas;* l. 75. *you deal in dangerous things*, seems intended to suggest a reference to George II., Queen Caroline, and Sir R. Walpole, as Persius was said, by his biographer Probus, to have meant Nero, Pers. Sat. 1. 119, Dryden's transl.:

'The reeds shall tell you what the poet fears,
　　King Midas has a snout and ass's ears.'

Pope perhaps followed Boileau, Sat. 9. 222 :

'J'irai creuser la terre, et comme ce barbier,
　　Faire dire aux roseaux par un nouvel organe,
　　Midas, le roi Midas a des oreilles d'âne.'

l. 80. *That secret to each fool, that he's an ass.* This is the thesis of Boileau's 4th Satire :

'l'homme le moins sage
　　Croit toujours seul avoir la sagesse en partage,
　　Et qu'il n'est point de fou qui par belles raisons
　　Ne loge son voisin aux Petites Maisons.'

ass. To be taken literally, not as the vulgarised metaphor which it has now become.

l. 85. *Codrus.* Since Juvenal, Sat. 1. 2, a traditional name for an inept poetaster.

l. 86. *Thou unconcern'd canst hear the mighty crack:* a parody on Addison, ap. Tonson, Miscellanies, 6. 119:

> 'Should the whole frame of nature round him break,
> He unconcern'd would hear the mighty crack.'

This line is selected by Pope, Martinus Scriblerus on the Art of Sinking, ch. 12, as an instance of bathos 'depending on one choice word that ends the line.' Cf. Hor. 3 Carm. 3. 6:

> 'Si fractus illabatur orbis
> Impavidum ferient ruinæ.'

l. 96. *Lost the arch'd eye-brow, or Parnassian sneer.* The *arch'd eye-brow* of the *peer*, which corresponds to the *Parnassian sneer* of the *poet,* expresses derision. Less properly, Gray has made it expressive of horror. Agrippina, 165: 'Things that, but whisper'd, have arch'd the hearer's brow, and riveted his eyes in fearful extasy.' Pope uses the expression again, Dunciad, 2. 5:

> 'Great Cibber sate; the proud Parnassian sneer,
> The conscious simper,' &c.

l. 99. *Bavius.* Since Virgil, Ecl. 3. 90, a traditional name for a wretched poet. Both Bavius and Codrus had been so employed by Young. Epistles to Mr. Pope, 1 and 2. Names originally belonging to real life come in time to stand as typical representatives of the moral qualities for which the persons were noted; e. g. Hector, Sat. and Ep. 1. 71, 'in a land of Hectors.'

l. 100. *Still to one bishop Philips seem a wit.* Ambrose Philips, a writer of popular verse, of various kinds. Philips's Pastorals had appeared in Tonson's Miscellany, in the same volume, the sixth, with Pope's Pastorals. The praise awarded to Philips by Addison and Tickell was felt by Pope as constructive depreciation of himself. This was the foundation of Pope's bitter antipathy to Philips. For the grounds of this hatred of Pope's, see Johnson, Lives of the Poets, A. Philips ; see also below, l. 179, note. The *bishop* was Boulter, 1719, Bishop of Bristol ; 1724, Archbishop of Armagh.

l. 112. *This prints my letters.* In 1726 a collection of Pope's letters to Cromwell was published by Curll. One of Pope's habitual manœuvres, on which he spent a good deal of thought and contrivance, was to get his letters published by other people, and to pretend displeasure.

l. 116. *I cough like Horace, and, tho' lean, am short.* Horace was short and fat. Sueton. Vit. Horatii : 'Habitu corporis fuit brevis et obesus.'

l. 117. *Ammon's great son one shoulder had too high.* Alexander the Great had his head inclined a little toward the left shoulder. Cf. Anstey, New Bath Guide, Letter 13 :

> ‘ Grew bolder and bolder,
> And cock’d up his shoulder,
> Like the son of great Jupiter Ammon.’

See Essay on Man, 1. 160, note.

l. 118. *Sir, you have an eye!* Warburton: ‘It is remarkable that amongst these compliments on his infirmities and deformities, he mentions his *eye*, which was fine, sharp, and piercing.’ The point of the irony was therefore missed by Warburton. Pope had a complaint of the eyes, for which he consulted Cheselden: see Life by Roscoe, 1737; and cf. Sat. and Ep. 3. 51:

> ‘ I’ll do what Mead and Cheselden advise
> To keep these limbs and to preserve these eyes.’

l. 125. *What sin to me unknown,* &c. Cf. Boileau, Sat. 9 :

> ‘ Quelle verve indiscrète
> Sans l’aveu des neuf sœurs vous a rendu poète ?’

l. 125, seq. This introduction of personal history, followed by a commemoration of his friends by name, is formed upon Ovid, Trist. 4. 10. 19, seq.

l. 128. *I lisp’d in numbers, for the numbers came.* Ovid, l. c. :

> ‘ Sponte sua numeros carmen veniebat ad aptos,
> Et quod tentabam dicere, versus erat.’

l. 130. *no father disobey’d.* Pope’s father used to encourage him in writing English verses. He was difficult to please, and would often send the boy back to new turn them. When at last satisfied, he would say, ‘ These be good rhymes.’

l. 135. The enumeration of the choice spirits for whose praise the poet cared, gives effect by its contrast with the herd who decried him. In this artifice Pope imitates Boileau (Ep. 7. 94), as Boileau had followed Horace (1 Sat. 10. 81).

Granville the polite. George Granville, created in 1711 Lord Lansdowne of Bideford. He ranked among the poets and wits of Queen Anne’s time. His poems are in Johnson’s Collection, with a life by Dr. Johnson. He died Jan. 30, 1735, about a fortnight after the publication of this Prologue.

l. 136. *knowing Walsh.* William Walsh had long been dead (died 1708). He had himself written poems which Johnson admitted into his Collection. Johnson says of him, ‘ He was not merely a critic or a scholar, but a man of fashion.’ He was one of the first to discover Pope’s merits, and to patronise the incipient poet. Pope says (Spence, Anecdotes, p. 20), ‘ I was with him at his seat in Worcestershire for a good part of the summer of 1705.’ Pope owed much to Walsh, and always acknowledged the obligation. See Essay on Man, Introd. p. 18; and cf. Essay on Criticism, 729 :

'Such late was Walsh, the Muse's judge and friend,
    Who justly knew to blame or to commend.'

l. 137. *Well-natur'd Garth.* Sir Samuel Garth, M.D. (died 1718), who, though a man of letters, was highly distinguished in his profession. He was author of The Dispensary, and had lived with Dryden, on whom he pronounced a Latin eulogium at the College of Physicians, of which he was President.

l. 138. *Congreve.* William Congreve, died 1729. His comedies are the wittiest in the language, his miscellaneous poetry feeble aud characterless. Johnson, Life: 'It cannot be observed without wonder that a mind so vigorous and fertile in dramatic composition should on any other occasion discover nothing but impotence and poverty.'

l. 139. *The courtly Talbot.* Charles Talbot, Duke of Shrewsbury, died 1718, after having filled some of the highest offices in the State. Cf. Sat. and Ep., Epil. 2. 79.

Somers. See Sat. and Ep., Epil. 2. 77.

Sheffield. John Sheffield, Duke of Buckinghamshire (died 1721), wrote Essay on Poetry, and other pieces. He was Dryden's first patron, and erected to him a monument and bust in Poets' Corner. Stanley, Memorials of Westminster Abbey, p. 304.

l. 140. *mitred Rochester.* Francis Atterbury, Bishop of Rochester and Dean of Westminster, died 1732. See Sat. and Ep., Epil. 2. 82. Pope here copies Gay:

'See Rochester approving nods his head,
    And ranks one modern with the mighty dead.'

l. 141. *St. John's self.* Lord Bolingbroke, Pope's greatest friend and patron: see Essay on Man, 4. 385, and note.

great Dryden's friends before. The parenthesis ought, grammatically, to refer only to *St. John*, but the plural *friends* must be taken to include all the foregoing names. Yet it is not true of all these persons that they were *Dryden's friends.* Swift, as is well known, was much the reverse. He would never forgive Dryden's sentence, 'Cousin Swift, you will never be a poet.' The friendship between Dryden and St. John was such as was possible between a youth of twenty-two and an old man of sixty-nine. The two anecdotes which Bolingbroke used to tell of his visits to Dryden, are among the most interesting which have been preserved of the poet.

l. 143. *Happy my studies, when by these approv'd!* Cf. Rochester, Poems (Chalmers, vol. 8. p. 250):

'I loath the rabble; 'tis enough for me
    If Sedley, Shadwell, Shephard, Wycherley,
    Godolphin, Butler, Buckhurst, Buckingham,
    Approve my sense.'

l. 146.   *Burnets, Oldmixons, and Cooks.*   The point of this line is to lower Bishop Burnet, who wrote 'History of my own Time from the Restoration to the Peace of Utrecht,' by ranking him with two writers of far inferior calibre.

Cooks.   The allusion is perhaps to Roger Coke's Detection of the Court and State of England, of which the first ed. was published in 1694, and a fourth in 1719. Mr. Mawbey, who knew Thomas Cooke of Braintree, commonly called 'Hesiod Cooke,' takes it for granted that the allusion here is to *him*, as he certainly was intended Dunciad, 2. 138 : 'Cooke shall be Prior, and Concanen Swift.'   But Pope's own note, on all the three names, in the present passage, speaks of 'authors of secret and scandalous history,' a description which is less applicable to Thomas Cooke.

l. 148.   *While pure description held the place of sense.*   Pope's early productions; Pastorals, 1709; Windsor Forest, 1713. Cf. Essay on Man, 4. 391 :

> '. . . . urg'd by thee, I turn'd the tuneful art
> From sounds to things, from fancy to the heart.'

l. 149.   *Like gentle Fanny's was my flow'ry theme.*   See note on Sat. and Ep. i. 6.   '*A painted meadow*, &c., is a verse of Mr. Addison' (Pope).

l. 151.   *Gildon.*   Gildon began the attack in 1714 by publishing A New Rehearsal, or Bays the Younger.   In his Complete Art of Poetry, 1718, he had studiously depreciated Pope.   Gildon and Dennis had been already coupled in the Dunciad, 3. 178.   In a letter to Swift, 1725, Pope speaks of the hatred entertained towards him by 'bad people,' specifying Gildon and Cibber.

ll. 159, 160.   *Pains, reading, study, are their just pretence,*
                   And all they want is spirit, taste, and sense.

The wits of all ages have despised the critics and scholars.   But the sentiment was most strongly developed during the century which followed the Restoration, 1660–1760.   The art of popular writing had been discovered, or imported from France, an art by which a subject could be dilated on without any real knowledge of it being possessed by the writer, or communicated to the reader.   This period has accordingly left us hardly any books of permanent value, and has very few names of men of learning to boast. One of the few which it has contributed to the beadroll of fame is that of the very Bentley, who is here ridiculed by Pope with his usual vanity and want of discernment.   Nor was it a momentary outburst of petulance.   He returned to the charge in the 4th Dunciad (1742), in the elaborate periods 189-238.   Pope was led astray by his implicit reliance upon Swift.   In the Tale of a Tub, Swift had to revenge his patron, Sir W. Temple, and with this view poured all the ridicule at his command upon Wotton and Bentley, especially the latter. Bentley's incomparable Dissertation on Phalaris appeared in 1699. But it was fifty years before the English public discovered that Boyle and his party had not been victorious in the controversy. Of all the poets, Blackmore is the only one whose sympathies were on the other side. See his sorry doggrel 'Satyr on Wit' (1700):

> 'As certain words will lunatics enrage,
>   So do but Locke, or books, or Bentley name,
>   The wit's in clammy sweats or in a flame.'

l. 166. *word-catcher.* Churchill, Rosciad, 1062 :

> 'I can't catch words, and pity those who can.'

l. 168. *Preserved in Milton's or in Shakespear's name.* Milton's Paradise Lost, edited by Bentley, 1732; and Shakspeare, by Theobald in 1733. Cf. Dunciad, 4. 211 :

> 'The mighty scholiast whose unwearied pains
>   Made Horace dull, and humbled Milton's strains.'

Sat. and Ep. 5. 103 :

> 'Not that I'd lop the beauties from his book,
>   Like slashing Bentley with his desperate hook.'

l. 179. *The bard whom pilfer'd pastorals renown.* The charge of plagiarism, which Pope here brings against Ambrose Philips, he had fastened on him more than twenty years before. Pope sent to the Guardian (April 27, 1713) an ironical comparison of his own Pastorals with those of Philips, in which he affected to give the preference to his rival. In this he said that Philips's Pastorals 'gave manifest proof of his knowledge of books.' But Philips's ideas were no further pilfered than that they were the stock-in-trade of all pastoral writers. Philips's Pastorals were a professed imitation of Spenser, as Pope's were of Virgil, and as Virgil's had been of Theocritus.

renown. Dryden, Religio Laici, 75 :

> 'Nor he whose wisdom oracles *renown'd.*'

l. 183. *He, who still wanting, though he lives on theft.* Warburton compares Boileau (Sat. 1. 15), 'Qui toujours emprunte, et jamais ne gagne rien.' But it is only by a mistranslation of the word 'gagne' that any resemblance can be produced. 'Gagne' in Boileau means 'earns.'

l. 186. *Means not, but blunders round about a meaning.* Mor. Ess. 2. 114 :

> 'For true no-meaning puzzles more than wit.'

And again, Epigram to James Moore Smythe :

> 'But there's no meaning to be seen.
>   Why that's the very thing I mean.'

l. 190. *Tate.* Nahum Tate died in the Mint (1715), in great indigence. He had been much employed as a contributor to the versions of the classical poets in collective volumes—'Translated by several hands'—which were much in vogue in his day. Pope's sneers at the translators as an inferior species inevitably remind us, that his own fortune and position had been secured by a translation of Homer, which he had sublet to 'several hands.'

ll. 193-214. These celebrated lines are at once a masterpiece of Pope's skill as a poet, and his base disposition as a man. They unite the most exquisite finish of sarcastic expression with the venomous malignity of personal rancour. They have less of antithesis and epigram than the character of Wharton, or the Duchess of Marlborough, and therefore more reality. Pope felt every stab, and gratified his temper by the pain he inflicted. The lines were not published till Addison had been dead eight years. They appeared first as a fragment in the Miscellanies of 1727; but they were finished as early as 1716, when, according to Spence, they had been sent by Pope to Addison himself. Pope had meditated each point for years, as the germs of some of them appear in a prose letter to Craggs in 1715. In the first copy, in 1727, the name was given—Addison. The substitution of Atticus in 1735 may perhaps be an indication that Pope was not without some sense of the outrage he was committing. The supposed provocation was a project for a rival—Whig—translation of Homer, the suggestion of which Pope attributed to Addison. For an account of the misunderstanding, see Carruthers, Life, p. 117; Macaulay, Essays, vol. 2; Life and Writings of Addison.

l. 198. *Bear, like the Turk, no brother near the throne.* Taken by Pope from Denham, On Fletcher's Works:

> 'Nor needs thy juster title the foul gilt
>   Of eastern kings, who to secure their reign,
>   Must have their brothers, sons, and kindred slain;'

but originally Lord Bacon's. He applied it to Aristotle's treatment of preceding philosophers. De Augment. 3. 4: 'Aristoteles, more Otto-mannorum, regnare se haud tuto posse putabat, nisi fratres suos omnes contrucidasset.'

l. 201. *assent with civil leer.* Macaulay, Essays, 2. 33: 'Addison had one habit which both Swift and Stella applauded, and which we hardly know how to blame. If his first attempts to set a presuming dunce right were ill-received, he changed his tone, "assented with civil leer," and lured the flattered coxcomb deeper and deeper into absurdity.'

l. 208. *and so obliging, that he ne'er oblig'd.* Macaulay, l. c.: 'One charge which Pope has enforced with great skill is probably not without foundation. Addison was too fond of presiding over a circle of humble friends. Of the other imputations which these famous lines convey, scarcely one has ever been proved to be just, and some are certainly false. That Addison was not in the habit of *damning with faint praise* appears from innumerable passages in his writings, and from none more than from those in which he mentions Pope. And it is not merely unjust, but ridiculous, to describe a man who made the fortune of every one of his intimate friends, as *so obliging that he ne'er oblig'd.'*

l. 211. *wits and Templars.* Stanhope, Reign of Queen Anne, p. 536: 'Into the pit (when Cato was brought out) there was poured by Steele a band of friendly and intelligent listeners from the Inns of Court. Another such band came from Will's Coffee-house, which was then to men of letters what the Athenæum is now.' It is to these that Pope referred, when he said that whenever Addison held forth—

> *Wits and Templars ev'ry sentence raise.*

raise = applaud. See Essay on Man, 3. 97, note.

l. 213. *Who but must laugh, if such a man there be?*
    Who would not weep, if Atticus were he!

C J. Fox, in Rogers's Recollections, p. 10: 'The last couplet is very faulty. Why *laugh* if there be such a man? Why *weep* if it be Atticus? The name cannot add anything to our regret.'

l. 215. *What tho' my name stood rubric on the walls.* Lintot usually adorned his shop, which was between the Temple gates and bore the sign of The Cross Keys, with titles of books in red letters. Cf. Dunciad, 1. 40:

> 'Hence Miscellanies spring, the weekly boast
> Of Curll's chaste press, and Lintot's rubric post.'

Gay, Trivia, 3, fin.:

> 'High rais'd on Fleet-street posts consigned to fame
> This work shall shine.'

Boileau, Sat. 9. 229:

> 'Que Billaine l'étale au deuxième pilier.'

The practice dated from a much earlier period of bookselling. Hall, Satire 5. 2:

> 'When Mævio's first page of his poesy
> Nail'd to a hundred postes for novelty.'

And Ben Jonson's Epigrams, ep. 3:

> 'Nor have my title-leaf on posts or walls,
> Or in cleft sticks advanced to make calls
> For termers.'

l. 218. *On wings of winds came flying all abroad.* A verse of Hopkins's version of Psalm 104.

l. 222. *No more than thou, great George! a birth-day song.* A sarcasm on the King's well-known contempt for literature. He, like his father, 'hated all boets and bainters.' Cf. Sat. and Ep. 5. 404:

> 'But verse, alas, your Majesty disdains!'

Swift, Works, 14. 439: Directions for Making a Birth-day Song.

l. 225. *Nor like a puppy, daggl'd through the town.* Thomas Cooke applied these lines to Savage, who was said to have lived in convivial familiarity with the town authors, and to have secretly supplied Pope with scandalous anecdotes about them. See Gent. Mag., 1791, December, p. 1093. Pope employs the simile again, Sandys' Ghost; Works, Roscoe, 6. 458:

> 'Like puppy tame, that uses
>   To fetch and carry, in his mouth,
>   The works of all the Muses.'

l. 230. There is no reason for doubting the tradition, not doubted by H. Walpole (Royal and Noble Authors, 4) or Johnson (Lives of the Poets), that Bufo was meant for Charles Montagu, Earl of Halifax. Roscoe's reasoning against it will not bear examination. Pope after having drawn him as Bufo in 1735, wrote of him in 1738, that he was 'a peer no less distinguished by his love of letters, than by his abilities in parliament,' a statement not inconsistent with the present character, perhaps even a stratagem of concealment. Until some other personage can be pointed out, to whom the lines on Bufo, including the last,

> He help'd to bury whom he help'd to starve,

can possibly apply, all answer to objections is unnecessary.

The character of Montagu, and his patronage of letters, is sketched in firm lines by Macaulay, Hist. vol. 5. p. 156, seq. He explains the seeming puzzle that a man who loved literature passionately, and rewarded literary merit munificently, should have been more savagely reviled both in prose and verse than almost any other politician in our history. In Faction Displayed (1706), Halifax figures as 'Bathillo.'

l. 233. *Fed with soft dedication all day long*, e. g. Addison's Epistle; Steele, Tatler, Dedication of vol. 4.

l. 236. *And a true Pindar stood without a head.* Cf. Juvenal, Sat. 8. 4.

l. 244. *And others, harder still, he paid in kind.* Gifford thought that Pope shadowed his Bufo in part from Juvenal, Sat. 7. 38 seq. But the resemblance, though marked in Gifford's translation, is faint in the original.

l. 245. *what wonder!* This interjection is intended to convey that the great poet disdained to join the throng of poetasters in toadying the Mæcenas. But Dryden belonged, in politics and religion, to the opposite party to that to which Montagu Earl of Halifax belonged. The best of the answers to Dryden's controversial poem, 'The Hind and Panther,' was written by Montagu in conjunction with Prior, 'The Hind and Panther transvers'd to the Story of the Country-mouse and the City-mouse,' 1687.

l. 246. *judging eye.* Imitated by Gray, Ode for Music, 71:

> 'Thy liberal heart, thy judging eye,
>   The flower unheeded shall descry.'

l. 247. *But still the great have kindness in reserve.* Scott, Life of Dryden, p. 471: 'It is seldom the extent of such a deprivation is understood, till it has taken place; as the size of an object is best estimated, when we see the space void which it had long occupied. The men of literature, starting, as it were, from a dream, began to heap commemorations, panegyrics and elegies; the great were as much astonished at their own neglect of such an object of bounty, as if the same had never been practised before; and expressed as much compunction as if it were never to occur again.'

l. 248. *He help'd to bury.* Stanley, Memorials of Westminster, p. 303: 'Lord Halifax offered to pay the expenses of the funeral, with £500 for a monument.'

help'd to starve. Inasmuch as he had not relieved his wants. Halifax may have not unreasonably thought that a Tory poet, and Catholic convert, a political convert too, might have had his wants supplied by his own party.

l. 258. *Neglected die, and tell it on his tomb.* Stanley, Memorials of Westminster, p. 315: 'Gay died at the house of the Duke of Queensberry, and was buried in the Abbey, 1732. . . . Lord Chesterfield and Pope were among the mourners. He had, two months before his death, desired "My dear Mr. Pope, whom I love as my own soul, . . . if a stone shall mark the place of my grave, see these words put upon it,

> Life is a jest, and all things shew it,
> I thought so once, and now I know it."'

The epitaph now inscribed on his monument was written by Pope.

l. 262. *To live and die is all I have to do.* This line is borrowed from Denham, Of Prudence:

> 'Learn to live well, that thou may'st die so too;
> To live and die is all we have to do.'

l. 265.   *Above a patron, tho' I condescend*
>   *Sometimes to call a minister my friend.*

These lines describe the relations which had been established between the wits and the politicians in the reign of Queen Anne. The writers and wits had raised themselves to equal consideration with the statesmen, in a way which had never been seen in England before. But it was too unnatural to last. The inauguration of Parliamentary government and systematic corruption by Walpole destroyed the influence for which the wits had been courted. At this time (1735) it was a thing of the past. Like so much else in this Prologue, e. g. the characters of Bufo and Addison, Pope is drawing upon his recollections, rather than describing the facts of the day. He belongs already to the past, both in style and matter. See Introd. p. 10.

l. 268. *believe, and say my prayers.* Cf. Gray, of himself:

> 'No very great wit, he believed in a God.'

l. 280. *Sir Will.* Sir William Yonge, Bart., Secretary at War 1735–1746. Cf. Sat. and Ep., Epilog. i. 68.

l. 280 *Bubo.* George Bubb Dodington, created, 1761, Lord Melcombe. The two are coupled again, Sat. and Ep., Epil. **I.** 68:

> 'The flow'rs of Bubo, and the flow of Yonge.'

Moral Essay, 4. 20. He is probably meant also, Moral Essay, **I.** 59:

> 'When universal homage Umbra pays,
>   All see 'tis vice and itch of vulgar praise.'

l. 283. *Curst be the verse,* &c. For the sentiment cf. Skelton, Colin Cloute, 1091:

> 'For I rebuke no man
>   That vertuous is, why than
>   Wreke ye your anger on me?
>   For those that vertuous be
>   Have no cause to say
>   That I speke out of the way.'

l. 299. *Who to the Dean and silver bell can swear.* Moral Essays, 4. 141: 'And now the chapel's *silver bell* you hear.' 4. 149: 'To rest the cushion and soft *Dean* invite.' The reference is to the description of Timon's Villa in the 4th Moral Essay. Pope wishes to insinuate that that description was imaginary. But it is impossible to doubt that by Timon's Villa he intended Canons. The denial was a part of his system, which is justly described by Mr. Carruthers, Life, p. 290: 'To equivocate genteelly, as he termed it, or to deny firmly, as circumstances might require, were expedients he never hesitated to adopt. Imaginary details being generally worked in to his pictures, he could always quibble, and deny part with truth.' Johnson, Life of Pope: 'From the reproach which an attack on a character so amiable brought on him, he tried all means of escaping. He was at last reduced to shelter his temerity behind dissimulation. He wrote an exculpatory letter to the Duke, which was answered with great magnanimity, as by a man who accepted his excuse without believing his professions.'

l. 300. *And sees at Cannons what was never there.* On the estate of Canons, near Harrow and Edgware, a magnificent mansion was built at a cost of £200,000, in 1712, by Mr. Brydges, created, in 1719, Duke of Chandos. He was the patron of art and learning in an age when they had ceased to be in repute, and when the great nobles were lavishing their wealth on electioneering contests. He contributed £200 towards the publication of Hudson's Josephus, and a like sum to Berkeley's Bermuda College. The place being too expensive for his successor, in 1747 Canons was pulled down. Cf. Gay, Epist. 4:

> 'If Chandos with a liberal hand bestow,
>   Censure imputes it all to pomp and shew;
>   When if the motive right were understood,
>   His daily pleasure is in doing good.'

l. 305. *Sporus.* John, Lord Hervey, son of the Earl of Bristol, personally attached to the Court of George II., in the capacity of Vice-Chamberlain. Pope hated this nobleman with a malignity beyond what can be accounted for by his being a Whig, and a favourite at Court. The first attack was in 1727, in the Miscellanies. In 1733 (Sat. and Ep. 1) he was again sneered at under the name of 'Lord Fanny.' To this Lord Hervey replied in Verses to the Imitator of Horace. Pope retorted, in a prose Letter to a Noble Lord (Works, Roscoe, 7. 397), which he followed up by the present character of Sporus. The name itself—that of one of Nero's minions—was designed as an insult, though it had been employed by Marston (1598), Sat. 1, without the insinuation. A full account of the feud between Pope and Lord Hervey is given by J. W. Croker, in his Introduction to Lord Hervey's Memoirs. He says, p. xliii., ' It is impossible not to admire, however we may condemn, the art by which acknowledged wit, beauty, and gentle manners, the Queen's favour, and even a valetudinary diet, are travestied into the most odious defects and offences.' But it seems questionable if the poet's virulence here be not an error in point of art, as it undoubtedly is an offence against public morality. The accumulation of odious epithets and disgusting images revolts the imagination and enlists our sympathy against the writer. Like all overcharged statements, it arouses mental resistance, and prompts disbelief. Only a knowledge of Lord Hervey's real character enables us to understand how much the distorted picture wants truth, but every reader feels how much it wants probability.

l. 319. *Or at the ear of Eve, familiar toad.* The allusion is to Milton. Lord Hervey was trusted and consulted by Queen Caroline, who governed George II. Familiar, used often in this sense by Milton, Par. Lost, 2. 219, 761; 11. 305.

l. 330.   *Eve's tempter thus the rabbins have exprest,*
                  A cherub's face, a reptile all the rest.
For the opinion that Eve's tempter was not any natural serpent, but Satan in a form half seraphic, half serpentine, see Mayer, Historia Diaboli, p. 218 (ed. 1780). And so, no doubt from Jewish tradition, in early Christian art. Though in the thirteenth century the serpent is generally represented with plain zoological characters, yet he sometimes appears with human head and arms. The head is sometimes that of a woman, sometimes that of a man. See Didron, Archéol. de l'Art, p. 74.

l. 349. *The blow unfelt.* The allusion is to a lampoon published in 1728, professing to give the tale of a whipping inflicted on Pope in Ham Walks. For a full account, see Carruthers, Life, p. 268. Pope confidently believed that Lady Mary Wortley Montagu was the fabricator of this story.

l. 351. *Th' imputed trash.* Pope notes on this: ' such as profane

Psalms, Court Poems, and other scandalous things printed in his name by Curll and others.' Dr. Johnson, however, and Mr. Carruthers, both think that Pope was author of a Roman Catholic Version of the First Psalm for the Use of a Young Lady, 1716, which was attributed to him at the time. Boileau makes a similar complaint of the trash that was fathered upon him. Ep. to Lamoignon:

> '. . Vient-il de la province une satyre fade,
> D'un plaisant du pays insipide boutade,' &c.

l. 353. *the pictur'd shape.* Warton: 'Hay, in his Essay on Deformity, has remarked that Pope was so hurt by the caricature of his figure, as to rank it among the most atrocious injuries he received from his enemies.' According to Fenton, Atterbury once said of his friend Pope, that 'there was a crooked mind in a crooked body.'

l. 354. *Abuse, on all he lov'd, or lov'd him, spread.* Carruthers, Life, p. 151: 'Curll the bookseller published every scrap which he could rake out of the sinks of literature against Pope and his friends.'

l. 363. *Japhet,* i.e. Japhet Crook, alias Sir Peter Stranger. Cf. Sat. and Ep., Epil. 1. 120: 'Shall Japhet pocket, like his Grace, a will;' and 'The Unparallel'd Impostor,' by James Moore (London, 1731).

l. 365. *Knight of the post.* Cunningham, Handbook of London, p. 543: 'Shameless ruffians who sought employment in Westminster Hall as hired witnesses, and walked openly, with a straw in their shoe to denote their quality.' Butler, 'Miscellaneous Thoughts:'

> 'Discharge all damages and costs
> Of knights and squires of the Post.'

Nash, Return of the Knight of the Post from Hell, 4to. 1606.

or of the shire. The opposite end of the social scale. The representative in Parliament of an English county, as distinguished from the representatives of the cities and towns, who are called burgesses.

l. 371. *friend to his distress.* Towards the close of his life Dennis was in distressed circumstances. The Provoked Husband was brought out at the Haymarket for his benefit, and Pope furnished a Prologue.

l. 374. *Full ten years slander'd, did he once reply?* Dennis' Character of Mr. Pope was published in 1716, and was perhaps the earliest of the libels upon him. The first Dunciad, bks. 1–3, which was Pope's *reply,* was published in 1728.

l. 375. *Three thousand suns* = poeticè, ten years, Welsted, it seems, had told two *lies.* One, that Timon's Villa meant the Duke of Chandos' seat at Canons. But the Fourth Moral Essay was written in 1731, and was apologised for, or the allusions disclaimed, immediately. This, therefore, is not the *lie* on which three thousand suns were suffered to go down. We must therefore, with Mr. Carruthers, refer the *lie* in question to Welsted's 'Triumvirate,' 1718. The story of this *lie*, of very small importance, which Pope avenges in the present line, may be read in Carruthers' Life, pp. 79–80.

lie. As to Pope's thus giving the lie to a living person (Welsted died 1748), we must remember that brutal language of that kind passed between Englishmen of that time more easily than it now does. An extreme case is furnished by Lady Cowper's Diary, 1715. Lord Townshend was sent to the Duke of Somerset by George I., to tell him he was dismissed. The Duke enquired the reason. Lord Townshend answered that he did not know. Then said the Duke, 'By God, my Lord, you lie; you know that the King puts me out for no other cause but for the lies which you and such as you have invented and told of me.'

l. 378. *Let Budgel charge.* Not imperative, but past tense indicative; = 'he suffered Budgel to charge.'

charge low Grub-street on his quill, i.e. charge Pope's pen with having been employed in contributing to the Grub-street Journal. Pope, in a note on this line, asserts that 'he never had the least hand, direction, or supervisal' of the paper. It is ascertained that he had frequently communicated paragraphs to it.

Grub-street. Johnson, Dict.: 'The name of a street in London, much inhabited by writers of small histories, dictionaries, and temporary poems, whence any mean production is called *Grub-street*.' It is now called 'Milton-street,' from its proximity to the Bunhill residence of the great poet.

l. 379. *except his will.* Budgel was charged by common repute with having forged the will of Dr. Matthew Tindal. See Sat. and Ep. 4. 64.

l. 380. *the two Curls.* Curll, the bookseller, and Lord Hervey. Lord Hervey is here coupled with the libellous bookseller, as above, l. 363, he was paired with Japhet Crook. On Curll, see Gay, Epist. 4:

'Were Prior, Congreve, Swift, and Pope unknown,
Poor slander-selling Curll had been undone.'

l. 385. *James Moore.* Son of Arthur Moore, and Fellow of All Souls College, Oxford; a friend of the Blounts of Maple-Durham, with whom he corresponded under the name of Alexis. See above, l. 23: 'Arthur, whose giddy son neglects the laws,' later known as J. Moore-Smythe.

l. 388. *Of gentle blood.* Pope claimed to be connected on the father's side with the Earls of Downe. The claim, founded only on family tradition, wants direct confirmation. It is, however, allowed by Mr. Hunter to be not in itself improbable. (See Hunter, Pope, his Descent and Family, 1857.) Dr. Bolton, Dean of Carlisle, said that Pope's grandfather was a clergyman in Hampshire. Mr. Hunter is inclined to identify him with Alexander Pope,

Rector of Thruxton, 1631. Pope's mother was daughter of William Turner, a Roman Catholic gentleman of Yorkshire.

l. 388. *part shed in honour's cause.* One of the Turners was killed, and another died, in the service of Charles I.

l. 391. *than Bestia's from the throne.* This allusion remains doubtful. In Sat. and Ep. 3. 90, *Bestia* stood in first ed. in place of D * l. The name is possibly from Horat. I Ep. 15. 37, where 'Bestius' stands for a rich miser.

l. 393. *Nor marrying discord in a noble wife.* Dryden, and after him Addison, had sought advancement by connecting themselves with noble families, but only reaped domestic unhappiness.

l. 397. *Nor dar'd an oath.* As a Roman Catholic he declined to take various oaths which were at that time necessary qualifications for civil offices.

l. 398. *no schoolman's subtile art.* The Jesuit Casuists had treated with great subtlety the theory of equivocal propositions, with especial reference to the test oaths imposed in this country. Strictly speaking the Casuists and the Schoolmen were two very different classes of writers. Cf. Dunciad, 4. 27:

> 'Morality, by her false doctrines drawn,
> Chicane in furs and casuistry in lawn.'

ll. 406-413. The pathetic sweetness of these concluding lines is not surpassed by anything else which Pope has written. Their effect is founded on the truth they express. Pope's filial piety is well attested, and the affectionate solicitude with which he surrounded the declining years of his aged mother held the leading place in his duties and occupations. He is, therefore, here expressing a sentiment genuine and deep. But mixed up with this, as seems inevitable in all that comes from Pope, is a strain of deception. (1) The lines as originally conceived, had another subject, and were afterwards altered and applied to Mrs. Pope. (See Letter to Aaron Hill, Sept. 3, 1731.) (2) When this Epistle to Arbuthnot was published, Mrs. Pope had been dead eighteen months. She died June 7, 1733. It was only by the fiction of supposing himself to have been composing the Epistle as far back as the first half of 1733, that he could speak of himself as 'rocking the cradle of reposing age.'

l. 417. *And just as rich as when he serv'd a queen.* Arbuthnot had been physician to Queen Anne, and had apartments in the Palace at St. James's. On the Queen's death, he had to leave these; and he writes to Swift, August 12, 1714: 'My case is not half so deplorable as poor Lady Masham's and several of the Queen's servants, some of whom have no chance for their bread, but the generosity of his present Majesty.'

SATIRES AND EPISTLES. I.

(Imitation of Horace, 2 Sat. 1.)

1733.

Pope told Spence, Anecdotes, p. 62: 'When I had a fever one winter in town, that confined me to my room for five or six days, Lord Bolingbroke came to see me, happened to take up a Horace that lay on the table, and in turning it over, dipt on the first satire of the second book. He observed how well that would suit my case, if I were to imitate it in English. After he was gone, I read it over, translated it in a morning or two, and sent it to press in a week or fortnight after. And this was the occasion of my imitating some other of the Satires and Epistles.'

This Satire was first published alone, in 1733, under the title 'Dialogue between Alexander Pope of Twickenham in com. Midd. on the one part, and the Learned Counsel on the other.'

To Mr. Fortescue. William Fortescue, a descendant of the celebrated Judge Sir John Fortescue, called to the Bar in 1715, was at this time Attorney-General to the Prince of Wales. He was intimate with the wits and literary men of the day, yet was not considered a bad lawyer. He is reputed to have written the case of 'Stradling v. Stiles' in the Memoirs of Scriblerus. He became Baron of the Exchequer in 1736, and Master of the Rolls in 1741. He must be distinguished from Sir John Fortescue (also a descendant of the illustrious chief justice of Henry VI.) who was at this time a judge in the Court of Common Pleas. Cf. Gay, Trivia, 2. 475:

'Come Fortescue! sincere, experienc'd friend,
  Thy briefs, thy deeds, and e'en thy fees suspend.'

l. 3. *wise Peter.* Peter Walter, who had acquired a very large fortune as attorney and money-scrivener. He was Clerk of the Peace for Middlesex, and, at this time, M.P. for Winchelsea, voting with the Court. He lived at Stalbridge, Dorsetshire, and Pope had been in the way of hearing about him when staying with Lord Digby at Sherborne. Peter Walter was the original of Peter Pounce in Joseph Andrews.

l. 4. *Chartres.* See Essay on Man, 4. 130, note.

l. 6. *Lord Fanny.* Cf. Sat. and Ep., Prol. 149: 'gentle Fanny,' i.e. Lord Hervey. Pope pretended that it was only the anglicised form of the Latin 'Fannius' (the 'ineptus Fannius' of Hor. 1 Sat. 10. 79), but his readers saw through the excuse which scarcely affected to be serious. See Sat. and Ep., Prol. 305, note.

a thousand such a day. It is said of Lucilius that he would dictate two hundred lines at one time. Ronsard boasted of being able to write two hundred lines before dinner, and as many again after.   Nisard, Lit. Franç. 2. 296.

l. 8.   *counsel*, 'council' in Warburton's ed. 1751, in ed. 1740, and in the original fol. 1733.   It must have been originally a clerical error.

l. 10.   *Advice, and, as you use, without a fee.*   Horace applies for advice to Trebatius, a lawyer, but who was also noted as a drinker and swimmer. Hence the point of his answers, which is lost in those put into the mouth of Fortescue.

l. 18.   *cowslip wine.*   Pope, Letter to Cromwell, 1708 : 'Well, for the future, I'll drown all high thoughts in the Lethe of cowslip wine.   As for fame, renown, reputation, take 'em critics !'

l. 20.   *Hartshorn.*   'Sirop of cowslep, and hartshorn' occur in a sleeping potion prescribed for Swift, 1733.   Scott, Life of Swift, p. 28.

l. 22.   *the bays.*   The insignia of the poet laureate.

l. 23.   *Sir Richard.*   Blackmore, knighted by William III., in 1697.   Cp. Sat. and Ep. 5. 387.

    rumbling, rough, and fierce.   See Blackmore's Poem on the Duke of Marlborough's Victories, 1706.

l. 27.   *Budgel.*   This is to punish Budgell for having suggested in The Bee, Feb. 1733, that Pope contributed to the Grub-street Journal.   Poor Budgell, who had been ruined, partly by powerful enemies, partly by South Sea speculation, was beneath Pope's notice.   But besides twice mentioning him in the present Satire (see l. 100), he returned to the attack in 1735. See Sat. and Ep., Prol. 378.   The name spelt by Pope, Budgel, is written by himself, Budgell.

l. 28.   *Paint angels trembling round his falling horse.*   Allusion to the Battle of Oudenarde, 1708.   It was begun by a charge of combined English and Hanoverian horse, in which the Prince of Hanover rode, and had his horse shot under him.

l. 30.   *Carolina.*   Queen-Consort of George II., a Princess of Branden-burg-Anspach.   During ten years she may be said to have governed England.   She was the especial object of hatred to the Tory opposition. though with the nation at large she was more popular than any other member of the royal family till George III.   See Stanhope, History of England, ch. 15.

l. 35.   *Cæsar scorns the poet's lays.*   Cf. Sat. and Ep., Prol. 222, note. Pope returns to the charge again, Sat. and Ep., Ep. 5. 404 :
                    'But verse, alas ! your majesty disdains.'
On the King's want of literature, cf. Lord Hervey's sarcasm, 'Ep. to the Queen,' Mem. vol. 2. p. 152 :
                    'For admittance to your eyes, I plead
                That some great princes certainly could read.'

l. 36. *It is to history he trusts for praise.* With Pope's sarcasm, cf. Boileau's flattery to Louis XIV., Épître 1:

> 'Qui mit à tout blâmer son étude et sa gloire,
> A pourtant de ce roi parlé comme l'histoire.'

l. 42. *A hundred smart.* Ben Jonson, Hor. 2 Sat. 1:

> 'In satire each man though untouch'd complains
> As he were hurt, and hates such biting strains.'

And cf. Phædrus, Fab. lib. 3. prol.

in Timon and in Balaam. Timon, Mor. Ess. 4. 99 seq.; Balaam, Mor. Ess. 3. 339 seq. Timon is ingeniously introduced here to back up his declaration that the Duke of Chandos was not intended.

l. 43. *The fewer still you name, you wound the more.* Pope says (Sat. and Ep., Prol., Adv.), 'Many will know their own pictures, there being not a circumstance but what is true; but I have for the most part spared their names, and they may escape being laughed at, if they please.' Cf. Gay, Shepherd's Week:

> ' . . . I no man call an ape, an ass;
> 'Tis his own conscience holds the glass.
> Thus void of all offence I write,
> Who claims the fable knows his right.'

l. 46. *Darty.* Charles Dartineuf, celebrated for his love of good eating, and, it should seem, as a joker: see Gay, Welcome from Greece, Ep. 6. A paper in The Tatler on Wine (No. 52) is by him. See Sat. and Ep., Ep. 6. 87.

l. 47. *Ridotta,* from Ital. *Ridotto* = a rout, an evening reception. Horace Walpole speaks of Ranelagh as 'a rout.' H. Walpole to George Montagu, 1769: 'There was what they called a "ridotto al fresco" at Vauxhall, for which one paid half a guinea, though except some thousand more lamps, and a covered passage all round the garden, there was nothing better than on a common night.' Cf. The Man of Taste (1733):

> 'In Lent, if masquerades displease the town,
> Call 'em Ridottos, and they still go down.'

And Byron, Beppo, st. 58:

> 'They went to the Ridotto; 'tis a hall
> Where people dance and sup, and dance again;
> Its proper name, perhaps, were a mask'd ball.'

l. 49. *F—— loves the senate.* Said by Bennett to mean Henry Fox, afterwards Lord Holland. But it does not appear that he entered Parliament till 1735. And in the first folio edition of 1733 there is no initial F., but only a blank. If the Fox brothers are meant, F—— must be Stephen, afterwards created Lord Ilchester, who entered the House of Commons in 1727. The brother who loved Hockley-hole would then be the more celebrated Henry Fox. They were both intimate friends of Lord Hervey, and as such reckoned by Pope among his enemies. Henry Fox once upbraided Lyttelton in the House with his intimacy 'with an unjust and licentious lampooner'—meaning Pope.

l. 49. *Hockley-hole.* Hockley-in-the-hole, near Clerkenwell-green, a place of public diversion, a kind of bear-garden, celebrated for its bear and bull baitings. Gay, Trivia, 2. 410:

> 'Behind him moves, majestically dull,
> The pride of Hockley-hole, the surly bull;
> Learn hence the periods of the week to name,
> Mondays and Thursdays are the days of game.'

The amusements of Hockley-hole are ridiculed in the Touch-stone, Essay 7 (1728); cf. Spectator, No. 436.

l. 50. *Like in all else as one egg to another.* Similarly Gay, Welcome from Greece:

> 'Another Simon is beside him found,
> Another Simon, like as straw to straw'—

of the two Harcourts, father and son.

l. 51. *I love to pour out all myself, as plain.* Boileau, Ép. 9. 57:

> 'Mon cœur toujours conduisant mon esprit
> Ne dit rien aux lecteurs qu'à soi-même il n'ait dit;
> Ma pensée au grand jour partout s'offre et s'expose.'

l. 52. *downright Shippen.* Coxe, Memoirs, 2. 316: 'Shippen and Sir R. Walpole had a personal regard for each other. He used to say, Robin and I are two honest men. He is for King George and I for King James; but those men with long cravats—meaning Sandys, Rushout, Gibbon, &c.—only desire places under King George or King James.' Shippen's honesty, however, was such as is compatible with his taking the oaths of allegiance to the family on the throne. Lord Campbell says, Chancellors, vol. 4. 419, 'Harcourt took the oaths upon the maxim which guided the conduct of "downright Shippen," and many other adherents of the Stuarts who were considered honourable men, that such oaths were not binding, and that the sin of taking or breaking them lay upon those who imposed them.' Marchmont Papers, 2. 246.

Montaigne. Montagne in Warburton's ed. 1751, and though not a press error, as it occurs again (e.g. Mor. Ess. i. 87, Sat. and Ep. 3. 26), it may be considered a clerical error.

l. 53. *as certain to be lov'd as seen.* Mor. Ess. 1. 54:

> 'Thus gracious Chandos is belov'd at sight;
> And ev'ry child hates Shylock, though his soul
> Still sits at squat, and peeps not from its hole.'

l. 66. *Erasmus.* Died 1536. Unable either to wink at the abuses of the

Church, or to approve the violence of Luther, Erasmus had the fate of being decried by both parties as a Latitudinarian, or indifferent in matters of religion.

l. 70. *To run a-muck.* Dryden, Hind and Panther, pt. 3. 1188:

> 'Frontless and satire-proof, he scours the streets,
>   And runs an Indian muck at all he meets.'

Scott notes, 'When a Malay has lost his whole substance by gaming, he intoxicates himself with opium, and rushes into the streets, crying, "Amocca," (kill), and stabbing every one he meets with his crease.'

l. 71. *in a land of Hectors.* The street bullies, who infested London by night, attacking foot-passengers and beating the watch, had at an earlier date passed under the slang name of *Hectors.* Shadwell, The Scowrers (1690): 'Pugh! this is nothing; why I knew the *Hectors,* and before them the Muns, and the Tityre Tus; they were brave fellows indeed.' Macaulay, History of England, 1. 282: 'At a later period arose the Nicker, the Hawcubite, and the yet more dreaded name of Mohawk. Milton was thinking of those pests of London, when he dictated, P. L. 1. 498:

> "And in luxurious cities, where the noise
>   Of riot ascends above their loftiest towers,
>   And injury and outrage, and when night
>   Darkens the streets, then wander forth the sons
>   Of Belial, flown with insolence and wine." '

l. 75. *Peace is my dear delight.* Cf. Sat. and Ep., Prol. 158:

> 'If wrong, I smil'd; if right, I kiss'd the rod.'

Fleury. Cardinal Fleury, at this time at the head of affairs in France. With the strongest desire to maintain the peace of Europe, his ministry was one of constant war. The War of the Polish Succession was only concluded by the Treaty of Vienna, 1738, when three years afterward broke out the War of the Austrian Succession. Fleury died 1743. See Voltaire, Siècle de Louis XV.

l. 81. *Delia's rage.* Delia is Lady Deloraine, widow of the first Earl Deloraine, and governess of the younger princesses. The gossip of the day charged her with having poisoned Miss Mackenzie. Lord Hervey, Mem. 2. 36, note.

l. 82. *Hard words or hanging, if your judge be Page.* Sir Francis Page, promoted to the King's Bench 1727, died 1741. He was known among his contemporaries as ' the hanging judge.' Without the abilities of Judge Jeffreys, he was deemed as cruel and as coarse. He tried Savage for the murder of Sinclair, and is said to have treated the prisoner with heartless insolence and levity. See Foss, Judges, 8. 143; cf. Dunciad, 4. 26; Sat. and Ep., Epil. 2. 159:

'Against your worship when had S—k writ?
Or Page pour'd forth the torrent of his wit?'

He was buried at Steeple-Aston, Oxfordshire, where a huge monument, by Scheemaker, still exists in the church.

l. 85. *Its proper power to hurt, each creature feels.* Cf. Swift:

'Brutes find out where their talents lie;
A bear will not attempt to fly.'

l. 89. *Walters.* The same name which Pope, who is very careless in this respect, writes 'Waters,' Mor. Ess. 3. 20, and 'Walter,' Sat. and Ep. 2. 168.

l. 100. *Lee.* See Sat. and Ep., Prol. 20.

Budgel. See Sat. and Ep., Prol. 378, note. Add Macaulay's harsh notice, Essays, 2. 338 : 'Budgell descended rapidly from one degree of vice and misery to another, ruined his fortune by follies, attempted to repair it by crimes, and closed a wicked and unhappy life by self-murder.'

l. 103. *plums.* Whitehead, Hunting Song, st. 4: 'The cit hunts a plumb, while the soldier hunts fame.' A 'plumb' or 'plum' = £100,000.

l. 107. *Dash.* Milton, P. L. 2. 114:

'His tongue
Dropt manna . . . to perplex and dash
Maturest counsels.'

l. 108. *Bare the mean heart that lurks beneath a star.* Rogers, Table-talk, p. 27 : 'Perhaps the best line Pope ever wrote!' It was after quoting this line that Rogers mentioned, by way of qualification, the munificence and promptitude, with which noble as well as simple had hastened to aid himself on occasion of the robbery of the Bank.

l. 112. *Flatt'rers and bigots.* Bigots in the Lutrin, as well as continually in the Satires. But no poetical flattery offered to Louis XIV. could be more gross than that of Boileau himself. See especially Épîtres, 1 and 8. Louis XIV. gave Boileau a pension of 2,000 livres as a reward for the adulatory lines which now stand as the hundred and forty last verses of Épître 1: 'Au Roi.' It was Boileau's own boast that he

'Dans ses vers pleins de sincérité
Jadis à tout son siècle a dit la vérité.'

l. 113. *Laureate Dryden.* Dryden succeeded Davenant as Poet-laureate in 1670. He was deprived at the Revolution as a Catholic, and succeeded by Shadwell.

fryar; i.e. the character of Father Dominic in The Spanish Friar. It was brought on the stage in 1681-2, and in the then excited temper of the nation, was received with rapture by the public, who thought that no villany in a Roman Catholic priest could be exaggerated. The play was prohibited during the reign of James II.

l. 116. *unplac'd, unpension'd.* Pope, as a Catholic, could not hold a place.

Halifax, and afterwards Craggs, offered him a pension out of the secret service money, which Pope declined. See full account of the circumstances, Spence, Anecdotes, p. 66.

l. 125. *There my retreat the best companions grace.* See Introd. p. 10.

l. 127. *St. John.* Bolingbroke was in England, at Dawley, for the ten years 1725–1735; in this last year he withdrew to France.

l. 129. *And he, whose lightning pierc'd the Iberian lines.* Charles Mordaunt, third Earl of Peterborough. Marlborough, with his usual sagacity, had discerned the latent genius for war which lurked in this eccentric man, 'the last of the Knights errant,' and had sent him to command in Spain. He died in 1735, and left Pope his watch, which had accompanied him in all his travels, and had been the gift of Victor Amadeus, Duke of Savoy. For character of Earl of Peterborough, see Macaulay, Essays, 2. 68; Stanhope, Hist. of Engl. 1. 520.

l. 130. *quincunx.* Called in Searle's plan of Pope's garden 'The Grove,' the trees being planted in regular order. In a *quincunx* the trees were planted by fives, four of them forming a square, and the fifth placed in the middle. The operation repeated again and again formed one continuous plantation. The *quincunx* was derived from the practice of the Roman vine-growers, and was in the seventeenth century a fashionable mode of planting groves, orchards, &c. Thomson had preceded Pope in the parallel, Autumn, 1072:

> 'What pity, Cobham, thou thy verdant files
> Of order'd trees should'st here inglorious range,
> Instead of squadrons flaming o'er the field,
> And long-embattled hosts.'

l. 131. *Or tames the genius of the stubborn plain.* An improvement of Gay, Fable 15:

> ''Tis mine to tame the stubborn plain,
> Break the stiff soil and house the grain.'

l. 132. *conquer'd Spain.* A poetical flight. The campaign alluded to by Pope, that of 1705–6, was indeed brilliant; and Peterborough received the thanks of the House of Lords for it. Yet in 1709, at the conferences for peace, it was found that the Bourbon prince, from whom we had *conquered Spain*, was king in nine-tenths of the country. All that remained of Peterborough's conquest was Catalonia.

l. 138. *This, all who know me, know; who love me, tell.* Spence, Anecdotes, p. 77: 'When I was telling Lord Bolingbroke that Mr. Pope on every catching and recovering of his mind, was always saying something kindly either of his present or absent friends, and that it seemed to me as if his humanity had outlived his understanding, Lord Bolingbroke said, "It has so; I never in my life knew a man that had so tender a heart for his particular friends, or a more general friendship for mankind." '

l. 145. *in Richard's times.* See Sat. and Ep. 5. 257, note.

l. 148. *Edwardi sext. or prim. et quint. Eliz.* Pope was fond enough of this low jingle effect to repeat it; Lines to Lord Bathurst:

> ' But if you will not take my word,
>   See anno quint. of Richard Third,
>   And that's a coppice call'd when dock'd.
>   Witness ann. prim. of Harry oct.'

It had been used in Hudibras, I. cant. 2:

>   ' · · · if 't be a drum
>   He'll sign it with Cler. Parl. Dom. Com.'

And imitated in Pleader's Guide:

> ' Are forc'd to cite opinions wise,
>   Crock. Car., Crock. Jacq., and Crock. Eliz.'

SATIRES AND EPISTLES.   II.

(Imitation of Horace, 2 Sat. 2.)

1734.

To Mr. Bethel. For account of him, see Essay on Man, 4. 126, note.

l. 5. *buffet.* Fr., naturalised in English, but pronounced as in Fr.; = sideboard. Its etymology is considered doubtful by Littré, Dict. s. v. It is perhaps same word as ' buvette,' from Lat. ' bibo.'

l. 6. *pride.* See Essay on Man, 2. 6, note.

l. 8. *mantling.* Milton, Par. Lost, 4. 258; 5. 279; Com. 294.

l. 9. *vers'd in schools.* See Essay on Man, 2. 81, note.

l. 10. *wise without the rules.* A literal rendering of Horace's ' abnormis sapiens,' = ' a philosopher outside the pale of any particular sect or school.'

l. 13. *your butler stroll'd abroad,* is the cause of the wine being locked up; and if the words *the river yet unthawed* are to be placed in parenthesis, ought to be so too.

l. 25. *Oldfield.* Warburton: ' This eminent glutton ran through a fortune of £1,500 a year, in the simple luxury of good eating.' Cf. Sat. and Ep. 6. 87:

> ' Hard task ! to hit the palate of such guests,
>   When Oldfield loves what Dartineuf detests.'

l. 26. *a whole hog barbecued.* Pope: ' A West Indian term of gluttony; a hog roasted whole, stuffed with spice, and basted with Madeira wine.'

l. 28. As a comment on this line the reader may refer to Lord Chesterfield's Works, 5. 199.

l. 39. *beccaficos.* A term of the market, not of ornithology, under which several species of the genus Sylvia are included. S. hortensis is migratory, and spends the summer in our island. Willoughby, Ornithology, says, 'Beccafigos abound in Candy and Cyprus, where they are salted in great numbers, and transported into other countries. With us, in England, they are called Cyprus-birds, and are in no less esteem with our merchants for the delicacy of their taste, than they were of old with the Italians.' King, Art of Cookery (1708), gives, as the English equivalent, 'Chats.' 'The chats come to us in April and breed, and about autumn return to Afric.'

l. 42. *Bedford-head.* A celebrated eating-house in Southampton-street, Covent-garden. Cf. Sober Advice:

> 'When sharp with hunger, scorn you to be fed
> Except on peachicks at the Bedford-head?'

l. 49. *Avidien, or his wife.* Mr. Edward Wortley Montagu and Lady Mary, according to Mr. Carruthers. Cf. Sat. and Ep. 6. 234:

> 'All Worldly's hens, nay, partridge, sold to town,
> His ven'son too, a guinea makes your own.'

Warburton naïvely remarks on this couplet, 'Our poet had the art of giving wit and dignity to his Billingsgate.'

l. 56. *or heard their son was drown'd.* The foolish and vicious conduct of their son was a severe distress to Lady Mary and Mr. Montagu. So incurable were his vicious propensities, that the wish falsely ascribed to them in the text would hardly have been unnatural, had it been true.

l. 60. *souse.* Johnson, 'to immerse in pickle.' Lord Hervey uses it in its metaphorical sense, Mem. 2. 150:

> 'And little Titch with lower scandal souse.'

l. 75, seq. This passage is quoted by Chesterfield in Common Sense, Feb. 11, 1738; a paper which may be read as an illustration of the present Satire (Works, 5. 197).

l. 88. *The sickness of long life, old age.* Wakefield: 'Ter. Phormio, 4. 1. 9: Senectus ipsa morbus.'

l. 101. *Lord Fanny.* See Sat. and Ep. 1. 6, note.

l. 119. *the new-built churches.* Stanhope, Reign of Queen Anne, p. 480: 'April, 1711, the Queen sent a message to the Commons recommending to them the supplying of new churches in the growing suburbs of London. In consequence of this, fifty new churches were directed to be built within the bills of mortality, computing 4,750 souls to each church. The cost was defrayed by the duty on coals.' Cf. Dunciad. 2. 27.

l. 119. *fall.* In 1732 some of these churches, being founded on boggy land, or run up by fraudulent contractors, were ready to fall.

l. 120. *repair Whitehall.* This charge, the neglect of the public buildings by the Whig ministry, Pope had urged before—Dunciad, 3. 327:

> 'See under Ripley rise a new Whitehall,
>
> While Jones' and Boyle's united labours fall.'

See Pope's note there.

l. 122. *As M**o's was.* Assumed by Warton to mean the Duke of Marlborough. 'The Duke of Marlborough's treasure,' writes Vanbrugh (to Tonson), 'exceeds the most extravagant guess. A round million has been moving about in loans on the land-tax,' &c.

five per cent. By statute of 12 Anne the rate of interest had been reduced to five per cent., though in the public funds it continued to exceed seven per cent. A member stated in the House of Commons, in 1717, that money could be obtained, on good security, at four per cent.

l. 129. *Thus Bethel spoke, who always speaks his thought,*
And always thinks the very thing he ought.

This is one of those couplets which betray their own artifice. The first line has been filled in after, and for the sake of, the second.

l. 133. *In South-sea days.* In 1711 the floating debt of the Treasury had reached the vast sum of ten millions. In order to provide for it, Lord Oxford, then at the head of the Treasury, incorporated the proprietors of these debts as a Company with exclusive right to trade to the South Seas.

l. 134.   *surmis'd*
The lord of thousands.

Pope had speculated in South-sea stock in 1720. It is not ascertained if he was a great loser. Johnson suggested that he only lost what he imagined himself to have gained. In a letter to Atterbury (Works, 7. 200, Roscoe's ed.) Pope speaks as if his loss had been considerable. Pope's pecuniary affairs have been minutely investigated by Mr. Dilke in the Athenæum, 1854.

now excis'd. Lord Hervey, Memoirs, 1. 159: 'That which gave rise to these commotions was a project of Sir R. Walpole to ease the land-tax of a shilling in the pound, by turning the duty on tobacco and wine, then payable on importation, into inland duties, i.e. changing the customs on those two commodities into excises. By this scheme, joined to the continuation of the salt duty, he proposed to improve the revenue £500,000.' There was already an excise on malt, salt, and spirits, which in 1733 produced over three millions. Walpole's proposal therefore was only one for the extension of an existing duty, not for the creation of a new excise.

l. 135. *In forest planted by a father's hand,* i.e. when he lived in Windsor Forest, where his father had purchased twenty acres of land.

l. 136. *five acres*, i.e. at Twickenham. Carruthers, Life, p. 170: 'The scene of the poet's operations was small, not much larger than his favourite model, the garden of Alcinous, which comprised four acres. But the Twickenham five acres ultimately boasted, amid their winding walks and recesses, a shell temple, a large mount, a vineyard, two small mounts, a bowling-ground, a wilderness, a grove, an orangery, a garden-house, a kitchen-garden.'

l. 137. *piddle.* Johnson, Dict.: 'To pick at table; to feed squeamishly and without appetite.' Pope, ap. Spence, Anecdotes, p. 29: 'When I fell into the method of translating thirty or forty verses of Homer before I got up, and *piddled* with it the rest of the morning, it went on cosily enough.' Sat. and Ep., Prol. 164: 'pidling Tibalds.' See also Guardian, No. 34. It was known as an expression peculiarly Pope's. As such it is introduced by Hawkins Browne into his parody on Pope, Pipe of Tobacco:

> 'Nor less the critick owns thy genial aid
> While supperless he plies the *piddling* trade.'

l. 152. *Tho' double tax'd.* In 1722 an Act was passed for raising £100,000 a-year from the estates of Roman Catholics and Nonjurors. The family of the Pendrills was specially excepted in consideration of the devotion of their house to Charles II. in his escape after the battle of Worcester.

l. 154. *standing armies.* The maintenance of a body of troops had been one of the points always in dispute between William III. and his Parliament. The cry against *standing armies* was revived by the Tory opposition for factious purposes, and was almost annually dilated on by their orators in the House. Pulteney, in 1732, had made a speech on the topic. The preamble to the Mutiny Act, still annually passed, embodies the phrase, and points to the old jealousy of the 'country party.'

l. 159. *sage Homer's rule.* Odyssey, 15. 74.

l. 166. *Vernon.* Mrs. Vernon, the proprietor of Pope's house and garden at Twickenham.

l. 172. *Twenty year.* Lord Hervey, Mem. 1. 280: 'Expedition was never reckoned among the merits of the Court of Chancery; but whilst Lord King presided there (1725–1733) the delays of it were insupportable.'

l. 175. *Shades that to Bacon could retreat afford.* Gorhambury, Hertfordshire, twenty-two miles from London. The house was built by Sir Nicolas Bacon in 1568. It is described by Pennant in his Journey from Chester, 1782. It was pulled down by Lord Verulam, in 1785, when the present house was built.

l. 176. *booby Lord.* William, first Viscount Grimston. Author of 'Love in a Hollow Tree,' a juvenile play, reprinted more than once by his enemies.

l. 177. *Helmsley.* 'Hemsley' in Warburton's ed., 1751, is an error. The estates in the parishes of Helmsley and Kirkby-Moorside, belonging to the Duke of Buckingham, were purchased by Sir Charles Duncombe, ancestor of Lord Feversham. The mansion, now called 'Duncombe Park,' was built in 1718, from designs by Vanbrugh.

SATIRES AND EPISTLES. III.

(Imitation of Horace, 1 Ep. 1.)

1737.

To Lord Bolingbroke. Horace's Epistle is addressed to Mæcenas. Lord Bolingbroke was at this time residing in France, having retired from political life, on finding that it was hopeless to make head against the power of Sir Robert Walpole.

l. 3. *sabbath of my days.* Born in 1688, Pope was now forty-nine.

l. 6. *See modest Cibber now has left the stage.* Ironical, Cibber having returned to the stage after a formal retirement in 1733.

l. 8. *Hang their old trophies o'er the garden-gates.* Warton has preserved the tradition that Pope's allusion was to the entrance to Lord Peterborough's lawn at Bevis Mount, near Southampton. Pope had paid his last visit to Bevis Mount in August 1735.

l. 9. *ev'n in Brunswick's cause.* Warburton's note on this deserves to be quoted, as showing how little the authorized commentator appreciated the irony of his author. He says, 'In the former editions it was *Britain's cause.* But the terms are synonymous.'

l. 15. *void of fire or force.* Cf. Sat. and Ep. 1. 27: 'With Budgel's fire and force.'

You limp, like Blackmore. Johnson, Life of Blackmore, says that Pope, who was always sneering at Blackmore, might have condescended to learn from him the art of reasoning in verse, which he needed much in his Moral Essays. Cf. Sat. and Ep. 1. 23, note.

l. 26. *And house with Montagne now, and now with Locke. Montagne,* so in ed. 1740, and in Warburton's ed. 1751. Another instance of Pope's carelessness in spelling proper names. Cf. Sat. and Ep. 5. 82, *Johnson* for *Jonson.* Horace's fluctuation between the rival sects, or opposed systems, of Epicureanism and Stoicism is not represented by Pope's *Montaigne and Locke,* between whom there is no incompatibility.

l. 29. *Free as young Lyttelton.* See Sat. and Ep., Epilogue 1. 47, note.

l. 40. *That lock up all the functions of my soul.* Not necessarily sleep, but all those hours in the twenty-four during which the life of the soul is not active. Pope used to tell of himself that he loved to escape from conversation to reading.

l. 45. *can no wants endure;* would mean in the language of our day 'cannot endure to want;' but in Pope's time it signified 'can want nothing.' Cf. Gay, Fable 13:

> 'Those who true love have ever try'd,
> No wants endure, no wishes make,
> But every real joy partake.'

l. 51. *Mead.* A distinguished physician then at the head of his profession. Mummius, Dunc. 4. 371, is said by Warton to be meant for Mead, but this must be a mistake.

Cheselden. Equally eminent as an anatomist, and an operating oculist. He was fond of the society of men of letters and learning, and saw much of Pope in his later years. An account, which he published in the Philosophical Transactions, 1728, of some experiments on a patient whom he couched for cataract, formed for a long time the leading case in the psychology of Sight and Touch.

l. 59. *Know there are rhymes, which fresh and fresh apply'd.* Wakefield: 'From Euripides, Hippol. 478. Euripides imitated Æschylus, P. V. 378.'

l. 68. *figure.* The verb is still common in this sense; the noun is only used in some phrases, as 'make a figure.'

l. 75. *long desires;* are, perhaps, 'desires which go great lengths.'

l. 82. *From low St. James's up to high St. Paul.* The contrast of High Church and Low Church came into use about the beginning of the century (1700), though the distinction of parties thus designated was essentially the same as that which had existed from the first establishment of the Church of England.

St. James's, i.e. the Court, patronised the Low Church party, who were staunch adherents of the Hanover family and the Protestant succession. At the Cathedral Church of St. Paul, the prebends being in the collation of the bishop of the diocese, Gibson, were mostly filled from the High Church party, while the Dean (Francis Hare), who was nominated by Government, was a Whig.

l. 83. *From him,* &c. From the lowest to the highest grade of those who deal with money.

l. 84. *notches sticks at Westminster,* i.e. in the Exchequer. The obsolete system of 'tallies' was still continued in this office down to 1831, long after the real business of finance had been transacted at the Bank of England. The Exchequer tallies were finally burnt, and in the process burnt down the Houses of Parliament. The office of 'Teller of the Exchequer' was lucrative, and much coveted. See The Humourist (1725), vol. 2. p. 223: ''Tis a fine thing to dance at Court in a birthday assembly; but not to me who had rather be swinging upon a gate in the country. Horace was an inimitable poet. Would I were a Teller of the Exchequer.'

l. 85. *Barnard.* Sir John Barnard, M.P. for London, and afterwards Lord Mayor, a conspicuous member of the Opposition or Country party.

l. 88. *As Bug now has, and Dorimant would have. Bug* = Lord Hervey, then Vice-Chamberlain. See Sat. and Ep., Prol. 309. *Dorimant* = George Bubb Dodington. See Sat. and Ep., Prol. 280. Dorimant is a character in Sir George Etherege's Man of the Mode, and was designed by the author for his own picture.

l. 89. *Barnard, thou art a Cit, with all thy worth.* Johnson, Life of Blackmore: 'In the early part of Blackmore's time, a citizen was a term of reproach.' Humourist, vol. 2. p. 176: 'Hard by stands a customer of inferior quality, a citizen's wife; who is reduced to the hard necessity of regulating her expenses by her husband's allowance, and is bursting with vexation to know herself restricted to lace of but fifty shillings a yard.'

l. 90. The first folio ed. has 'Bestia and Bug, their honours, and so forth.'

their honours. Fielding, Tom Jones, bk. 8. ch. 2: 'There is narrow a one of all those officer fellows but looks upon himself to be as good as arrow a squire of £500 a-year. To be sure it doth me good to hear their men run about after 'um crying "your honour," and "your honour." Marry come up with such honour, and an ordinary at a shilling a head.'

l. 98. *jargon.* Wedgwood, Dict.: 'Properly the chattering of birds, Fr. *jargonner,* to gaggle as a goose. Hence figuratively, an utterance of sounds not understood.'

l. 106. *And foremost in the circle eye a king.* Lord Hervey's Memoirs describe the rivalry between the German and the Italian Opera which grew, in 1734, as serious an affair as that of the Greens and Blues at Constantinople. The Court was Handelist; the King and Queen sate freezing at the empty Haymarket Opera, while the Prince with the Tory nobility filled that of Lincoln's-Inn-Fields.

l. 112. *honest S*z.* Augustus, eldest son of Baron Schutz, had been equerry to George II. when Prince, and became Master of the Robes, and Privy Purse to him, as King. He was a general favourite at Court. Mrs. Schutz was one of the Queen's Ladies-in-Waiting, and Miss Schutz accompanied the Princess Royal to Holland as one of her Maids of Honour.

l. 128. *some farm the poor-box.* A society had been chartered by Queen Anne under the title of the 'Charitable Corporation,' with the object of lending money to the poor upon pledges. In 1731 some of the officers embezzled half a million of its funds, and such numbers were ruined that Parliament was compelled to interfere. A lottery of £500,000 was allowed for the relief of the sufferers, and those of the managers who were members of the House were expelled.

l. 159. *aboard,* so rightly Warb. ed. 1751 ; but in earlier editions *abroad.*

l. 162. *My wig all powder, and all snuff my band.* Carruthers, Life, p. 408: ' Like Dryden, Pope took snuff. But when he went abroad or received company he was as particular and precise in his dress as he was in his poetry.'

l. 173. *Hale.* Richard Hale, M.D., spoke the Harveian oration 1724. Spence, Anecd. p. 60: 'I shall be very glad to see Dr. Hales, and always love to see him, he is so good and worthy a man. Only he has his hands so much imbrued in blood.—What ! he cuts up rats, aye, and dogs too !' Not to be confounded with Dr. Stephen Hale, the ' plain Parson Hale ' of Mor. Essays, 2. 198.

SATIRES AND EPISTLES. IV.

(Imitation of Horace, 1 Ep. 6.)

1737.

To Mr. Murray. William Murray, afterwards Chief Justice of the King's Bench, and Earl of Mansfield. He was at this time a young man of thirty-two, and a rising lawyer, who dallied with literature, and affected the acquaintance of the wits. Pope reckons him among the young friends, by whom he endeavoured to repair the gaps which time had made in his circle : ' There is a Lord Cornbury, a Lord Polwarth, a Mr. Murray, and one or two more.' To Swift, May 17, 1739.

l. 4. *Creech.* From whose translation of Horace, first published 1684, the two opening lines are taken.

l. 5. *congregated ball.* If a conjecture may be hazarded as to the possible meaning of this epithet, it = ' condensed, conglomerated.'

l. 31. *Parian charms.* Not a happy imitation of Horace's ' marmor vetus.' The frigidity is in the word ' charms,' a frigidity which is not produced by the ' Parii lapides ' of Virgil ; Georg. 3. 34.

l. 42. *Sigh, while his Chloe, blind to wit and worth,*
 Weds the rich dulness of some son of earth.
Lord Campbell, Chief Justices, 2. 339 : Murray ' was attached to a young lady of beauty, accomplishments, and birth, and she listened favourably to his suit. But her family, requiring a sight of his rent-roll, were not contented that her jointure and pin-money should be charged upon his rood of ground in Westminster Hall, and married her to a squire of broad acres in a midland county.' He afterwards married Lady Elizabeth Finch, daughter of the Earl of Winchilsea.

l. 49. *Grac'd as thou art, with all the power of words,*
 So known, so honour'd, at the house of Lords.
It seems incredible that Pope could have allowed this piece of bathos to

escape from his pen. The specimen of anticlimax given in Scriblerus, Art of Sinking (Roscoe, 5. 257),

> 'And thou, Dalhousie, the great God of war,
>   Lieutenant-Colonel to the Earl of Mar,'

is not more ridiculous than that here committed by Pope himself. It was parodied by Hawkins Browne:

> 'Persuasion tips his tongue whene'er he talks,
>   And he has chambers in the King's Bench Walks.'

l. 49. *at the House of Lords.* Observe the preposition. Young Mr. Murray was laying the foundation of his great reputation by pleading, on Scotch appeals, at the bar of the House of Lords, in which he afterwards, as Lord Mansfield, himself took the leading place.

l. 50. *another yet is nigh.* Alluding to the proximity of Westminster Abbey to the House of Lords.

l. 52.   *Where Murray (long enough his country's pride)*
              Shall be no more than Tully, or than Hyde.

Fulfilled in the year 1793. Stanley, Mem. of Westminster Abbey, p. 286: 'Lord Mansfield and Sir W. Follett are the only representatives of the legal profession buried in the Abbey.'

Shall be no more than, is ironical; but in such a connection irony is not in place.

l. 56. *Ward.* A quack who professed to cure, among other diseases, madness, by his pills of 'pulvis antimonialis.' His name is of constant recurrence in the squibs of the time. Sat. and Ep. 5. 182:

> 'Ward tried on puppies and the poor his drop.'

Bolingbroke wished Pope to consult him in 1744, when Pope was failing.

l. 61. *Cornbury disdains.* Afterwards Lord Hyde. Spence, Anecd. p. 59: 'On Lord Hyde's return from his travels, his brother-in-law, Lord Essex, told him, with a great deal of pleasure, that he had got a pension for him. Lord Hyde's answer was, "How could you tell I was to be sold; or how could you know my price so exactly?"'

l. 63. *Tindal.* Matthew Tindal, D.C.L., Fellow of All Souls' (died 1733), *denied* a Church in his treatise, The Rights of the Christian Church asserted against the Romish and all other Priests, &c., 1706. He was very far from *denying virtue.* On the contrary, his thesis that Christianity is only a republication of the religion of nature, lays an exclusive stress on virtue. The allusion in the words *denies virtue,* is probably not to any moral theory, but to the loose conduct attributed to Tindal. Cf. Dunciad, 2. 399:

> 'Toland and Tindal, prompt at priests to jeer.'

l. 82. *Anstis.* Garter King-at-Arms.

l. 85. *Timon.* The Duke of Chandos probably meant. Cf. Sat. and Ep., Prol. 300, note.

confounds = 'profusely lavishes.'

l. 112. *Up, up, cries Gluttony; 'tis break of day.* Wakefield: 'Dryden, Transl. of Persius, Sat. 5: Up, up, says Avarice, thou snor'st again.'

l. 126. *If, after all, we must with Wilmot own.* John Wilmot, Earl of Rochester. The passage quoted by Pope is in Letter to Artemisia (Chalmers, 8. 242):

> 'That cordial drop heav'n in our cup has thrown
>   To make the nauseous draught of life go down.'

SATIRES AND EPISTLES. V.

(Imitation of Horace, 2 Ep. 1.)

1737.

To Augustus. Augustus was one of George the Second's baptismal names. Lord Hervey, Mem. i. 305: 'Not that there was any similitude between the two princes besides their names. George Augustus neither loved learning nor encouraged men of letters, nor were there any Mæcenases about him. There was another essential difference between the two Augustuses; as personal courage was the only quality necessary to form a great prince, which the one was suspected to want, so I fear it was the only one the other was ever thought to possess.'

l. 1. *sustain the balanc'd world,* &c. The irony of this opening address was sufficiently patent to Pope's contemporaries. The modern reader must, in order to realise it, recall the insignificant figure which George II. made in the government of England.

As to foreign affairs, whatever weight this country possessed on the Continent was due to the statesmanship of Sir Robert Walpole, seconded by the Queen. The King comprehended nothing of them, but looked solely to the particular interests of the Electorate. After 1730, Sir Robert found it necessary to control the foreign affairs, as well as the home, which were his more peculiar province. As to *Arts,* George the Second's indifference and ignorance were proverbial. See Lord Hervey, Mem. vol. 2, for the story of his banishing a number of paintings by the old masters from Kensington, and filling their place with wretched modern daubs.

l. 2. *open all the Main.* In 1737 heavy complaints were made by the city of London merchants of what they called the 'depredations' of the Spanish cruisers. The fact was, the merchants were interfered with, by the vessels of war, in a profitable, but illicit, trade with the Spanish settlements. See the case stated by Burke, First Letter on a Regicide Peace, Works,

8. 145. Bowles explains *open all the Main*, that 'the King was so liberal as to leave it open to the Spaniards.' It means rather 'open it to British commerce.' Ironically, because it was what was not done. The grievance was that a fleet had not been despatched to the West Indies to enable the merchants to smuggle with impunity. *The Main* is short for The Spanish Main. By this term English sailors understood that part of the mainland of South America which belonged to Spain. Its use for 'the ocean' is wholly poetical.

l. 16. *Finds envy never conquer'd, but by death.* Cf. Waller, Panegyric:
'But living virtue, all achievements past,
Meets envy still to grapple with, at last.'

l. 29. *Wonder of Kings!* &c. The obligation to keep near the original Latin covers the sneer here concealed, which without the protection of Horace on the opposite page becomes too palpable.

l. 38. *And beastly Skelton heads of houses quote.* I have no doubt that Pope refers to a fact, but the *quotation* was either made in conversation, or if in print, has not been detected. A reprint of Marshe's edition of Skelton's Workes, 1568, had appeared in 1736. Pope says (Spence, Anecdotes, p. 87), 'Skelton's poems are all low and bad, there is nothing in them that is worth reading.' But the epithet *beastly* is inappropriate; yet, says Mr. Dyce (Skelton, i. 6), 'it has cast a blight on Skelton's reputation from which it has hardly yet recovered.'

l. 40. *Christ's Kirk o' the Green.* A humorous Scottish poem, almost certainly of the early sixteenth century; ascribed in the unique MS. to James I of Scotland, probably by error for James V.

l. 41. *the Devil.* The 'Devil' tavern between Temple Bar and the Middle Temple gate. The sign was taken from the legend of St. Dunstan, the house being nearly opposite the church of St. Dunstan. Here Ben Jonson lorded it with greater authority than Dryden did afterwards at Will's, or Addison at Button's.

l. 62. *courtesy of England*, is restricted in law to the single case of not disturbing the husband in the enjoyment, for his life, of his wife's estate, after her death. Pope applies it loosely to the case of not disturbing the claim of a poet to rank as a classic where a prescriptive title of a full century could not be made out.

l. 66. *look in Stowe*, i.e. in his 'Annales or General Chronicle of England,' which was the most popular collected history of our country during the seventeenth century, and till superseded at the beginning of the eighteenth by Echard, Rapin, Carte, and others. Stowe's 'Annales' went through a succession of editions between 1573 and 1720. It is not very properly referred to on the present occasion, as it makes scarce any mention of literature. Stowe is mentioned disrespectfully by Donne, Sat. 4:

> 'More than ten Hollinsheads, or Halls, or Stows,
> Of trivial household trash he knows.'

l. 75. *Cowley.* Abraham Cowley, died 1667. His epic was the Davideis. His Pindaric Odes profess to be an 'imitation of the style and manner of the Odes of Pindar.' Pindaric Odes, at one time greatly in fashion, had now fallen into such disrepute that Pope could speak of the best of them as forgotten. Gay in his instructions for the composition of a Miscellany, directs (Epist. 14)—

> 'Tire not our patience with Pindaric lays,
> Those swell the piece, but very rarely please.'

The Odes of Collins, published 1746, and those of Gray, 1757, were very coldly received by the public.

l. 78. *But still I love the language of his heart.* Pope, ap. Spence, Anecd. p. 95: 'Cowley is a fine poet in spite of all his faults.' And so, long after Pope; Cowper, The Task, book 4:

> 'I studied, priz'd, and wish'd that I had known
> Ingenious Cowley! . . . courtly though retir'd,
> Though stretch'd at ease in Chertsey's silent bowr's,
> Not unemploy'd, and finding rich amends
> For a lost world in solitude and verse.'

l. 80. *What boy but hears the sayings of old Ben.* Jonson had been dead exactly a century in 1737, yet his mots were still repeated by tradition in the coffee-houses. The only printed record of them is his Conversations with Drummond, whom he visited at Hawthornden in 1619, walking on foot to Scotland for the purpose.

l. 82. *Johnson's art—Shakspear's nature.* Pope again, Dunciad, 2. 223:

> 'To move, to raise, to ravish ev'ry heart,
> With Shakspeare's nature, or with Jonson's art.'

This was the current criticism of the Caroline age. Denham, on Fletcher's Works:

> 'Yet what from Jonson's oil and sweat did flow,
> Or what more easy nature did bestow
> On Shakspeare's greater name.'

Milton has stamped the contrast between 'Jonson's learned sock' and Shakspeare's 'wood-notes wild' (L'Allegro, 132), in words which will perpetuate the criticism as long as the language lasts.

Johnson; so in ed. 1751. The name was spelled either 'Johnson' or 'Jonson' indiscriminately by the poet's contemporaries, though it should seem that he himself wrote it 'Jonson.' See Notes and Queries, 3rd Series, 8. 195.

l. 84. *How Beaumont's judgment check'd what Fletcher writ.* These opinions are not Pope's. They are intended as characteristic of the random judgments of the public. 'Interdum vulgus rectum videt, est ubi peccat.'

l. 85. *How Shadwell hasty, Wycherley was slow.* The allusion is to Rochester (Chalmers, 8. 249) :

> 'Of all our modern wits none seem to me
> Once to have touch'd upon true comedy,
> But hasty Shadwell and slow Wycherley.'

Pope adds a note to his own line: 'Nothing was less true than this. But the whole paragraph must be taken for the common chat of the pretenders to criticism.' Rochester meant, as Warburton observes, 'not to design the difference of their talents, but the number of their productions.'

l. 86. *Southern.* Thomas Southerne, 1660–1746, wrote ten plays, of which only two obtained stage celebrity—Isabella ; or, The Fatal Marriage, and Oroonoko. Hallam says he was the first English writer who denounced the traffic in negro slaves.

Rowe. Nicholas Rowe, 1674–1718, Poet Laureate. His Fair Penitent and Jane Shore kept possession of the stage for a century. He is one of the few Whigs whom Pope has named without tacking to his name some depreciating epithet.

l. 87. *These, only these, support the crouded stage.* We may ask why Otway is omitted, who exerted more power over the passions than either Rowe or Southerne, and whose Venice Preserved was oftener produced than any piece of theirs, especially as Pope treats him so well below in ll. 277, 278.

l. 88. *eldest Heywood.* John Heywood, died ? 1580,—*eldest,* to distinguish him from Thomas Heywood, a dramatic writer of the time of James I. John Heywood's Interludes are a species of composition between the Moralities and the Drama.

l. 91. *Gammer Gurton.* 'Gammer Gurton's Needle' is the title of a dramatic piece which was supposed to be the earliest specimen of English comedy, until the discovery of 'Ralph Royster Doyster.' Its authorship is uncertain. It was probably produced about 1565, for acting by the students at Cambridge.

l. 92. *Careless Husband.* By Colley Cibber in 1704 ; a piece so superior to his other plays, that he was said to have had the assistance of Arthur Maynwaring in writing it. The origin of the suspicion however seems to have been a statement in Giles Jacobs' Poetical Register, 1723, a statement which is corrected in the Errata at the end of the volume.

l. 97. *Spenser himself affects the obsolete.* The language of Spenser (died 1599) is not the English of his own time, nor of any time, but an artificial archaism affected for the sake of effect. Ben Jonson said of him that 'he writ no language.'

l. 98. *And Sidney's verse halts ill on Roman feet.* English hexameters were attempted by Sir Philip Sidney (died 1586) in the Arcadia, book I:

> 'Lady, reserv'd by the heav'ns to doe pastors companie honor,' &c.

l. 100. *sweeps*. Observe how the antithesis is injured by the use of the word *sweeps*, which when said of movement denotes majesty. The word wanted was 'creeps on,' but the metre would not admit it. Dryden had said, 'Mac-Fleckno,' 'Or swept the dust in Psyche's humble strain.'

l. 104. *slashing Bentley*. Cf. Sat. and Ep., Prol. 164, note.

desperate hook. It seems obvious to understand this, as most of the commentators do, of the bill-hook of the hedger with which he slashes, or plashes, the quick fence. Notwithstanding, having in view Pope's note on Dunciad, 4. 194, I think that Warburton may be right in interpreting it of the *hooks*, or brackets in which Bentley enclosed lines he chose to declare spurious.

l. 106. *hates whate'er he read at school*. The allusion is to some lines of Lord Hervey, entitled 'Letter to a Doctor of Divinity,' in which he pleads that he

> '. . . long
> Had taken leave of Greek or Latin song,
> All that I learn'd from Dr. Friend at school,
> By Gradus, Lexicon, or Grammar-rule,
> Has quite deserted this poor John-trot head,
> And left plain native English in its stead.'

l. 107. *wits of either Charles's days*. Dug. Stewart, Elements, 3. 235: 'Wit is commonly regarded as one of the elements of poetical genius. So intimate is the connection between them, that by the authors of Queen Anne's reign poets were very generally called "wits."' Below, 179:

> 'We wake next morning in a raging fit,
> And call for pen and ink to show our wit.'

l. 108. *The mob of gentlemen who wrote with ease*. Cf. Prior's sarcasm (Chalmers, 10. 133):

> '. . . the world agrees
> That he writes well, who writes with ease,
> Then he, by sequel logical,
> Writes best, who never thinks at all.'

Pope, ap. Spence, Anecd. p. 105: 'Lord Dorset and Lord Rochester should be considered as holiday writers, as gentlemen that diverted themselves now and then with poetry, rather than as poets.'

l. 109. *Sprat*. Thomas Sprat, became, 1684, Bishop of Rochester, died 1713. In his youth he published some academical verses, of which the principal are, To the Memory of the Lord Protector, and The Plague of Athens. In the latter, he enumerates among the sufferers the Pythagoreans and the Stoics. Of Cromwell's fame he says that, 'like man it will grow white, as it grows old.' Yet for the enlightened interest he took in literature and learning, he has been complimented by having his verses included in the Collections of British Poets. Pope, ap. Spence. Anecd. p. 116, calls him 'a worse Cowley.'

l. 109. *Carew.* Thomas Carew, died 1639, has left only short occasional pieces. The longest is a mask, entitled 'Cœlum Britannicum.' He holds an intermediate place between the frigid affectation of the poets of the Restoration and the impassioned fantasy of the Elizabethan amatory poetry.

Sedley. Sir Charles Sedley, died 1701, was so highly applauded for his taste and judgment that Charles II. said, 'Nature had given him a patent to be Apollo's viceroy.' He effaced his brilliant endowments by conduct which was esteemed indecent even in that licentious age. Dryden in dedicating one of his plays to Sedley, describes 'the genial nights of mingled discourse and raillery' passed in his society. See Scott's Dryden, Works, 4. 351.

l. 110. *miscellanies.* Volumes under this title in which the smaller pieces of the popular poets of the day were collected. Among the more celebrated of these collections are the Miscellanies of Pope and Swift, 3 vols., 1727. Gay, Ep. 14, gives Bernard Lintot a receipt for the composition of such an olio to rival Tonson's :

  'As when some skilful cook to please each guest,' &c.

l. 113. *Or lengthen'd thought that gleams through many a page.* This characterises the best versifiers of the Restoration period, even Dryden. Their habit of composition was to take any idea, and play variations upon it, through any number of verses. Pope followed the opposite, or classical method, viz. to reduce a given meaning to its shortest expression.

l. 119. *On Avon's bank, where flow'rs eternal blow.* Carruthers, Life of Pope: 'Pope's Preface to his Shakspeare, published in 1725, must be pronounced inferior to Johnson's, but it is what no other author of the day, after Addison's death, could have written. Remembering the generally low appreciation of Shakspeare, Pope will not be found deficient in reverence and admiration.'

l. 120. *If I but ask, if any weed can grow.* Pope, Pref. to Shakspeare: 'One cannot wonder if Shakspear, having no other aim in his writings than to procure a subsistence, directed his endeavours to hit the taste and humour that then prevailed. The audience was generally composed of the meaner sort of people, therefore the images of life were to be drawn from those of their own rank, tradesmen or mechanicks. In tragedy nothing was so sure to cause admiration as the most strange and unnatural incidents, the most exaggerated thoughts, the most bombast expression, the most pompous rhymes, and thundering versification. In comedy nothing was so sure to please as mean buffoonery, vile ribaldry, and unmannerly jests of fools and clowns.'

l. 122. *Betterton—Booth.* Betterton, died 1710, was the leading actor of Dryden's age, and Booth (died 1733) of Pope's. Booth acted Cato when it was first brought out in 1712.

l. 127. *the former reign* = the reigns of the sovereigns before George's age.

l. 132. *Merlin's prophecy.* A collection of Prophecies in Latin, which had great currency in the Middle Ages, was circulated under the name of Merlin. Thomas Heywood published these 'Predictions in English, and their truth made good by our English annals,' 1641. Merlin, Prophet and Enchanter, is a purely fictitious personage, the creation of romance. But he was transferred to history by Geoffrey of Monmouth, who places him in the reign of Vortigern, tells how he defeated the Saxons at the Mons Badonicus, and transported Stonehenge out of Ireland to Salisbury plain. The English metrical romance of Merlin is extant, and was printed by Wynkyn de Worde in 1510.

l. 142. A line adapted from 'Lansdowne's Progress of Beauty' (Chalmers, 11. 21):

> 'From the loud palace to the silent grove
> All, by the King's example, live and love.'

ll. 149, 150. One of Pope's happiest couplets. Warton compares Antipater (Anthol. Græca, 2. 103. Jacobs): Ἡ τακεραῖς λεύσσουσα κοραῖς μαλα-κώτερον ὕπνου.

l. 153.
> *On each enervate string they taught the note*
> *To pant.*

The first Operas brought on the stage in England were produced by Sir W. Davenant at his theatre in Charterhouse-yard, which he opened in spite of the Puritan government in 1656.

l. 183. *Radcliff's doctors.* John Radcliffe, M.D., died 1714, founded his Fellowships in University College, Oxford, for Masters of Arts entered on the Physic line, tenable for ten years, 'the half of which time, at least, they are to travel in parts beyond sea for their better improvement.'

l. 186. *Ripley.* Ripley was patronised by the government, hence Pope's sneer. Ripley built Houghton for Sir Robert Walpole, and Wolterton for Lord Walpole; also the Admiralty in Whitehall. Cf. Dunciad, 3. 327:

> 'See under Ripley rise a new Whitehall,
> While Jones' and Boyle's united labours fall.'

See Sat. and Ep. 2. 120, note.

l. 195. *Flight of cashiers.* Knight, cashier to the South Sea Company, escaped to France, carrying with him the secret register called 'the green book.' The cashier of the Charitable Corporation, George Robinson, M.P. for Marlow, absented himself in October, 1731.

l. 211.
> *Or virtue or religion turn to sport,*
> *To please a lewd or unbelieving Court.*

Cf. Scott, Marmion, canto 1, Introd.:

> 'And Dryden in immortal strain
> Had rais'd the Table Round again,
> But that a ribald king and court
> Bade him toil on to make them sport;
> Demanded for their niggard pay,
> Fit for their souls, a looser lay,
> Licentious satire, song, and play.'

l. 214. *Roscommon.* Wentworth Dillon, Earl of Roscommon, died 1684. Besides occasional pieces, he translated Horace, Art of Poetry, and wrote An Essay on Translated Verse.

l. 215. *excuse some courtly stains.* Warburton told Spence that Pope meant this of Addison's Lines to the Princess of Wales, 1714. In these Addison appears to take credit for his Cato as a political play, though, while the Tory administration seemed firmly seated, he had displayed the greatest anxiety to have it considered neutral.

l. 221. *Let Ireland tell how wit upheld her cause.* Scott, Life of Swift Works, I. 274: 'From these studies the Dean was roused in the year 1720, and again appeared on the stage as a political writer, no longer the advocate of a ministry, but the undaunted and energetic defender of the rights of an oppressed people. No nation ever more needed a patriotic champion than Ireland at this period. The power of legislating for Ireland was assumed by the English Parliament, and it was so exercised as to fetter, as far as possible, the commerce of the kingdom.' Among other things the importation of Irish wool into England was prohibited.

l. 224. *The rights a court attack'd, a poet sav'd.* Bennet says that for this passage the author was threatened with prosecution.

l. 226. *Stretch'd to relieve the idiot and the poor.* Swift's resolution to endow a hospital for lunatics was taken many years before his death. Cf. his Verses on his own Death, Works, 14. 369:

> 'He gave the little wealth he had
> To build a house for fools or mad.'

With the first £500 he could call his own he instituted a fund for granting small loans to such industrious artisans and tradesmen as could find security for repayment by weekly instalments.

l. 228. *And stretch the ray.* Awkward substitute for Lucretius' 'Vitai lampada tradunt.'

l. 230. *Hopkins and Sternhold.* This passage is ironical, but the irony is not very transparent. 'Hopkins and Sternhold,' with Pope, are typical names for bad poets. Cf. Pope to Swift, October 15, 1725: 'My name is as bad a one as yours, and hated by all bad poets, from Hopkins and Sternhold to Gildon and Cibber.' The version of the Psalms which goes under their name is the joint contribution of seven or eight different versifiers. Thirty-seven Psalms 'drawen into English metre by Thomas Sternholde' were published in 1551.

l. 251. *ill-inclin'd* = 'having received an ill tendency or direction.'

l. 257. *At length, by wholesome dread of statutes bound.* There was an enactment against libel as early as the thirteenth century. It is Stat. Westminst. i. c. 34, 3 Edw. I., and was occasioned by a lampoon written seven years before upon Richard, King of the Romans. The verses may be seen in Percy's Reliques. To this case Pope alludes (Sat. and Ep. 1. 146):

'It stands on record that in Richard's times
A man was hang'd for very honest rhymes.'

But we do not find much in the Year-Books till the great case De Libellis Famosis, 3 James I., which was the foundation of what was considered, in Pope's time, law with respect to libels. See Barrington on the Statutes, p. 58.

l. 259. *warp'd.* Warp = a hawser, maritime term. To warp = to change the situation of a vessel by means of hawsers. Milton, P. L. 1. 341:

'A pitchy cloud
Of locusts warping on the eastern wind.'

l. 263. *We conquer'd France, but felt our captive's charms.* Notwithstanding De Quincey's (Works, 10. 49) witty protest, there is sufficient truth in Pope's assertion to allow it to represent Horace's 'Græcia capta ferum *victorem cepit.*' The cast and tone which English poetry assumed after the Restoration is French, and that by direct influence and communication. It is true that this communication was in no connexion with the conquest of France two hundred years earlier. But the same objection lies against Horace's antithesis. Greek literature was adopted and imitated by the Romans quite independently of the subjugation of Greece. If we allow 'Græcia capta victorem cepit' as a rhetorical contrast, not as cause and effect, we may allow Pope's transfusion, 'We conquer'd France, but felt our captive's charms.'

l. 267. *Waller was smooth.* Edmund Waller, died 1687. Johnson, Life of Waller: 'Waller certainly very much excelled in smoothness most of the writers who were living when his poetry commenced. But he was rather smooth than strong; of the "full-resounding line" which Pope attributes to Dryden he has given very few examples. The critical decision has given the praise of strength to Denham, and of sweetness to Waller.' Cf. Pope, Essay on Criticism, 360:

'Where Denham's strength and Waller's sweetness join.'

Dryden says, 'Well-placing of words for the sweetness of pronunciation was not known till Mr. Waller introduced it.' On this criticism, Masson observes (Essays, p. 102): 'To aver with such specimens of English verse before us as the works of Chaucer and Spenser, and the minor poems of

Milton, that it was Waller that first taught us sweetness or smoothness or even correctness of verse, is so ridiculous that the currency of such a notion can only be accounted for by the servility with which small critics go on repeating whatever one big critic has said.'

l. 267. *join:* i. e. unite the four things which follow. Cf. Churchill, Apology (Chalmers, 14. 284):

> ' With strong invention, noblest vigour fraught,
> Thought still springs up and rises out of thought,
> Numbers ennobling numbers in their course,
> In varied sweetness flow, in varied force ;
> The pow'rs of genius and of judgment join,
> And the whole art of poetry is thine.'

l. 269. *The long majestic march, and energy divine.* This magnificent tribute to the memory of Dryden must be limited to the language and expression. The ideas of Dryden are the thoughts of a bare and prosaic age, and not even its best thoughts. But there is an energy of expression, a force of reasoning, and a general sense of power about his lines, which distinguish him from all his contemporaries, and which are hardly to be found elsewhere in English poetry. Wakefield observes that Gray wrote his lines on Dryden with a reminiscence of Pope's expressions. Progress of Poesy, 104.

l. 271. *splay-foot verse.* Cf. Essay on Criticism, 354 :

> ' Then at the last, and only, couplet fraught
> With some unmeaning thing they call a thought,
> A needless Alexandrine ends the song.'

Though ridiculed by Pope and Swift, the Alexandrine long kept its place in English heroic verse.

l. 279. *And fluent Shakspeare scarce effac'd a line.* Ben Jonson, Discoveries (ed. Gifford, 9. 175) : ' I remember the players have often mentioned it as an honour to Shakspeare, that in his writing, whatsoever he penned, he never blotted out a line. My answer hath been, "Would he had blotted a thousand !"'

l. 287. *Congreve—Farquhar—Vanbrugh.* The best criticism on the Comic Dramatists of the Restoration is to be found in Macaulay's Essay on the subject.

Congreve. See Sat. and Ep., Prol. 138, note.

Farquhar. Born at Londonderry 1678, died 1707, æt. 29. His most successful play was ' The Beaux' Stratagem,' which held its place on the stage for more than a century.

Vanbrugh. Born 1666, died 1726. Cunningham, Lives of the Architects, &c., 4. 253 : ' No man who has been satirised by Swift and praised by Reynolds could have much chance of being forgotten ; but the fame

of him who was at once the author of " The Relapse," and " The Provoked
Wife," and the architect of Castle Howard and Blenheim, stands inde-
pendent of even such subsidiaries.'

l. 289. *How Van wants grace, who never wanted wit.* It is not certain
whether *grace* here is said of style and manner, or of an influence which
should have restrained the licence of his dialogue and situations. Pope uses
it frequently in this sense. Sat. and Ep. 6. 286 :

> ' My heir may sigh, and think it want of *grace*,
> A man so poor would live without a place.'

Of Sir John Vanbrugh Hallam says, Lit. of Europe, 3. 528 : ' Amanda, in
The Relapse, is the first homage that the theatre had paid since the Restoration to female chastity. Notwithstanding the vicious tone of the other
characters, in which Vanbrugh has gone as great lengths as any of his
contemporaries, we perceive the beginnings of a reaction which gradually
reformed the moral standard of the stage.'

l. 290. *The stage how loosely does Astræa tread.* Astræa, the poetical
name, parisyllabically, of Aphara Behn, died 1689. She was a prolific
authoress, having produced, besides novels, seventeen plays, which were
mostly successful. By *loosely* is indicated the indecorous character of some
of her performances.

l. 292. *And idle Cibber, how he breaks the laws,* i.e. the received laws of
the dramatic writers.

l. 293. *To make poor Pinky eat with vast applause.* William Pinkethman, a comic actor, called by Gildon ' the flower of Bartholomew Fair,
and the idol of the rabble.' It was in the character of Don Lewis, in
' Love makes a Man,' that Pinkethman ate two chickens in three seconds.
Pinkethman's name is prefixed to a collection of Jests published in
1720-1. See an account of him in Colley Cibber, Apology for his own
Life, p. 159. On the vulgar taste for theatrical pantomime, see Dunciad,
3. 265 :

> ' But lo! to dark encounter in mid-air
> New wizards rise; I see my Cibber there;
> Booth in his cloudy tabernacle shrin'd,
> On grinning dragons Cibber mounts the wind.'

l. 312. *Taste, that eternal wanderer, which flies.* Cibber, Apol. for his
own Life, p. 79 : ' Taste and fashion with us have always had wings, and
fly from one public spectacle to another so wantonly that a famous puppet-
shew in Salisbury Change, then standing where Cecil-street now is, so far
distressed these two companies [the King's and the Duke's], that they
petitioned the king for relief against it. Nor ought we to think this strange,
when Terence himself reproaches the Roman auditors of his time with the
like fondness of the rope-dancers.' Hecyra, Prol. ·

> ' Ita populus studio stupidus in funambulo
>   Animum occuparat.'

l. 313. *From heads to ears, and now from ears to eyes.* The downward course of taste from the acted, to the musical, drama, in the last generation, and from Operas to Pantomime in the present.

l. 318. *Old Edward's armour beams on Cibber's breast.* Cibber, Letter to Mr. Pope, 1742, defends himself from having been 'an encourager of these fooleries.'

l. 328. *on Orcas' stormy steep.* Pope explains in a note, ' the farthest northern promontory of Scotland, opposite to the Orcades.' In placing wolves in Scotland he seems to have forgotten his own note on Pastorals, Summer, 83. There he says, he withdraws the line, 'And list'ning wolves grow milder as they hear,' on account of ' the absurdity of introducing wolves into England.' Yet it was not so absurd as Pope supposed. The last wolf recorded to have been seen in Scotland was killed in 1743, in the parish of Moy (Inverness), by Macqueen, laird of Pollochock. See Notes and Queries, 2nd Ser., 8. 402.

l. 331. *Quin.* Quin's characters are enumerated by Churchill, Rosciad, 944. Quin held the first place as a tragic actor till the appearance of Garrick in 1741. He retired from the stage in 1753.

l. 334. *Booth enters.* According to Theophilus Cibber, Life of Booth, p. 68, Booth used to defend pantomime on the ground of its being the only means of keeping up the regular theatres against the superior attractions of the Opera. For Booth, see Sat. and Ep. 5. 122.

l. 348. *this part of the poetic state.* The drama as a distinct part of the poetical republic. Augustus' patronage was limited to the dramatic poets, and Horace puts in a petition for an extension of it to the other classes of poetry.

l. 352. *Or who shall wander where the Muses sing ?* The point of these four lines is obscure. It must be sought in Pope's desire to drag in, without regard to the context, a sneer at the Queen. *Merlin's Cave* was a whim of hers in Richmond Old Park, which cost her a good deal of money, and occasioned her constant vexation from the King. The selection of the books in the small library in the Cave did not please Pope, as it did not include his own writings, or those of his friends. The change of taste in the next generation was fatal to Merlin's Cave. Its destruction is commemorated by Mason, Heroic Epistle, l. 55 :

> ' . . . for see untutor'd Brown
> Destroys those wonders which were once thy own.
> Lo, from his melon-ground the peasant slave
> Has rudely rush'd and level'd Merlin's Cave,

> Knock'd down the waxen wizard, seiz'd his wand,
> Transform'd to lawn what late was fairy-land,
> And mar'd with impious hand each sweet design
> Of Stephen Duck and good Queen Caroline.'

l. 375. *As once for Lewis, Boileau and Racine.* Boileau, Ep. 10. 107:

> ' Que ce Roi, dont le nom fait trembler tant de Rois,
> Voulut bien que ma main craionnât ses exploits.'

Boileau was associated with Racine for the purpose of writing the history of the glories of Louis XIVth's reign in October, 1677.

l. 379. *Fit to bestow the Laureat's weighty place.* A sarcasm on Sir Robert Walpole, who had degraded the laureateship by bestowing it on Cibber as a reward for a political play—The Nonjuror.

l. 381. *Assign'd his figure to Bernini's care.* Bernini, born at Naples, 1598, was painter, sculptor, architect. He executed busts of a number of exalted personages, and amongst others of Charles I. and Louis XIV. His bust of Charles I. is not known to be in existence. It is conjectured that it may have perished in the fire of Whitehall. Bernini died in 1680. Pope possessed a head of Homer by Bernini, which he left by will to Lord Mansfield.

l. 382. *And great Nassau to Kneller's hand decreed.* Godfrey Kneller, a native of Lübeck, died 1723, is described in Pope's epitaph in Westminster Abbey as—

> ' Now for two ages having snatch'd from fate
> Whate'er was beauteous or whate'er was great.'

His great picture of William III. on horseback is now in the presence-chamber at Windsor.

l. 387. *One knighted Blackmore.* Sir Richard Blackmore was knighted by William III. in his professional character, as Physician in Ordinary, not as a tribute to his poetical merits. But his fame came from his poetry. Smith, Poem to Memory of John Philips, calls Blackmore—

> ' A haughty bard to fame by volumes raised,
> At Dick's and Batson's, and through Smithfield prais'd.'

one pension'd Quarles. This may have been a fact known to Pope by tradition. No authentication of it has yet been discovered. See Notes and Queries, 1st Ser., vols. 1 and 2.

l. 389. *No Lord's anointed but a Russian bear.* No altogether satisfactory explanation has yet been offered of this allusion. The difficulties of it are thus stated in Notes and Queries, 2nd Ser., 1. 449: 'The puzzle is how Ben Jonson and Dennis could concur on the same affidavit; why the *Lord's anointed* should be contrasted with a *Russian bear;* and why a *Russian* bear?'

l. 395. *your arms, your actions, your repose to sing.* The irony of these concluding lines was only too transparent in 1737. They now no longer speak for themselves. Their force will only be felt by those who have obtained some acquaintance with the life of George II. and the history of his reign. It must be observed that they were written before the war of the Austrian succession and the battle of Dettingen.

l. 413. *Praise undeserv'd is scandal in disguise.* Wakefield: 'From a Poem in Tonson's Miscellany, 1709.'

l. 418. *flutt'ring in a row.* The Odes and Poems of the time were brought out on broad sheets, or stitched pamphlets, folio size, which we may suppose pinned on the iron railings of Soho Square. This Square, built in 1681, was in 1737 still occupied by the nobility and gentry. Sir Roger de Coverley, 'when he is in town lives in Soho Square' (1711).

SATIRES AND EPISTLES. VI.

(Imitation of Horace, 2 Ep. 2.)

1737.

l. 1. *Dear Colonel.* Sir Clement Cotterel, Knt., Master of the Ceremonies, who assumed the name of Dormer on succeeding to the estate of Rousham, Oxfordshire. He died 1758. In 1735 we hear (Spence, Anecdotes) of Pope passing through Oxford on his way to Colonel Dormer's at Rousham.

Cobham's. Richard Temple, created Viscount Cobham, 1718, at whose seat at Stowe Pope was a frequent visitor. He was one of the deserters from Walpole's majority, and was punished for his vote against the Excise by the loss of his regiment and other places. Some account of him may be found in Glover's Memoirs, p. 7; and see Thomson, Autumn, 1072.

l. 24. *Sir Godfrey.* See Sat. and Ep. 5. 382. Having made a fortune by portrait painting, Sir Godfrey Kneller acted as Justice of the Peace at his country seat, Whitton, near Twickenham, and decided, Pope says, 'much in the manner of Sancho Pancha.'

l. 43. *Gave him much praise, and some reward beside.* Bennet: 'Evidently glancing at the Duke of Marlborough's avarice.'

l. 52, seq. With these interesting biographical details compare Sat. and Ep., Prol. 388–405.

Bred up at home, &c. Pope's education was, he told Spence, 'extremely loose and disordered.' The family priest, named Bannister, taught him grammar, following the plan adopted in the Jesuit schools, of teaching the rudiments of Latin and Greek together. He then attended two inferior schools at which he learned nothing. When he was twelve years old his father removed to Binfield, Berkshire. 'Considering (Spence, Anecdotes) how very little I had when I came from school, I think I may be said to have taught myself Latin, as well as French and Greek ; and in all these my chief way of getting them was by translation.'

l. 56. *To hunt for truth in Maudlin's learned grove.* Magdalen College, Oxford, to which two of Pope's intimate friends belonged—Robert Digby, and Thomas Warton, sen., afterwards (1718-1728) Professor of Poetry.

l. 59. *Depriv'd us soon of our paternal cell.* Wakefield refers this to orders from government for the removal of Papists to a certain distance from the metropolis.

l. 64. *For right hereditary tax'd and fin'd.* The penalties incurred by the Catholics and by the Non-jurors were distinct. Pope's father incurred them both. See Sat. and Ep., Prol. 397.

l. 72. *Years following years, steal something ev'ry day,*
   At last they steal us from ourselves away.
S. Rogers, Table-talk, p. 27: 'These lines, which Lord Holland is so fond of hearing me repeat, are as good as any in Horace himself.'

l. 79. *That turn'd ten thousand verses.* This seems to refer to the translation of Homer. But it is not even an approximation to the quantity of versification achieved by Pope. The Iliad alone contains, in the Greek, 15,790 lines.

l. 100. *A hackney-coach may chance to spoil a thought.* Smollett, Roderick Random (1748), ch. 13: 'While we were deliberating, a hackney coachman driving softly along, and perceiving us standing by the kennel, came up close to us, and calling, "A coach, master!" by a dexterous management of the reins made his horses stumble in the wet, and bedaub us all over with mud. After which exploit, he drove on, applauding himself with a hearty laugh, in which several people joined.'

l. 112. *Blackmore himself.* Johnson, Life of Blackmore: 'His residence was in Cheapside (No. 142), and his friends were chiefly in the city. In the early part of Blackmore's time a citizen was a term of reproach; and his place of abode was another topic to which his adversaries had recourse in the penury of scandal. He was accused of writing to the rumbling of his chariot wheels.'

l. 117. *seven years compleat.* Twenty-eight Terms residence and study, or *seven years complete*, were formerly required by the University of Oxford for the degree of M.A.

l. 132. *And shook his head at Murray as a wit.* Lord Campbell, Lives of Chief Justices, 2. 565: 'The absurd cry, that he (Lord Mansfield) knew no law, gained countenance only from the envy of the vulgar, who are always eager to pull down to their own level those who soar above them, and, in our profession, will insist, that if a man is celebrated for elegant accomplishments he can have no law, and if he is distinguished as a deep lawyer, that he can have no elegant accomplishments.'

l. 140. *Stephen.* Stephen Duck, Queen Caroline's Librarian at Richmond Lodge. See Sat. and Ep. 5. 352, note.

you and me, i.e. Theobald and Cibber. Cf. Sat. and Ep. 5. 352, note.

l. 143. *My dear Tibullus!* Cf. Reimer, Reime Dich (1763): 'Nenne diesen einen Flemming, er wird dich wieder einen Opitz rufen.'

l. 157.   *But how severely with themselves proceed*
          The men, who write such verse as we can read?
Cf. Boileau's account of his own laborious method of composition, Sat. 2.

          ' Mais mon esprit tremblant sur le choix de ses mots,
           N'en dira jamais un, s'il ne tombe à propos;
           Et ne saurait souffrir qu'une phrase insipide
           Vienne à la fin d'un vers remplir la place vide;
           Ainsi recommençant un ouvrage vingt fois,
           Si j'écris quatre mots j'en effacerais trois.'

Waller had first pointed attention to this great defect of English writing, Prol. to Maid's Tragedy:

          ' But faultless writing is th' effect of care.
           Our lines reform'd, and not composed in haste,
           Polisht like marble, would like marble last;
           But as the present so the last age writ;
           In both we find like negligence and wit.'

l. 162. *Nay, tho' at Court, perhaps, it may find grace.* In Horace, 'inter penetralia Vestæ.' This seasoning with opposition politics is not known to Horace; it is a foreign element introduced by Pope.

l. 166. *Bright through the rubbish of some hundred years.* Cf. the saying of Leibnitz regarding the Latin schoolmen, 'qu'il y a encore de l'or dans ces scories.' Nouv. Ess. p. 397.

l. 171. *Pour the full tide of eloquence along.* Cf. Gray, Progress of Poesy, l. 7:

          ' Now the rich stream of music winds along.'

l. 173. *Rich with the treasures of each foreign tongue.* Pope is not recommending a mixture of English, French, Italian, &c., but the equal employment of both elements of the English language. Coleridge, Table Talk, 2. 94.: 'It may be doubted whether a composite language like the English is not a happier instrument of expression than a homogeneous one like the German. We possess a wonderful richness and variety of modified meanings in our Saxon and Latin quasisynonymes, which the Germans have not. For "the pomp and prodigality of heav'n," the Germans must have said the "spendthriftness." '

ll. 178–9. *But ease in writing flows from art, not chance,*
As those move easiest who have learn'd to dance.

Quoted by Pope from himself, Essay on Criticism, 362–3, with a slight alteration. *Ease in writing* is meant of the style, not of the labour which it costs the writer, which are in inverse proportion to each other.

l. 184, seq. Cf. Boileau's version of the story, Sat. 4, 'Jadis certain bigot,' &c. It is characteristic of their respective countries that Boileau uses an ecclesiastical, and Pope a political setting.

l. 200. *There is a time when poets will grow dull :* i.e. a time of life after which the mind stiffens, and is no longer fertile of poetical imagery, or susceptible of poetical emotion. See Wordsworth, Preface to Poems.

l. 205. *And keep the equal measure of my soul.* The contrast intended seems to be that between the staid sobriety of prose, and the afflatus of the poet, which hurries him he knows not whither. But if so, the couplet, *I'll e'en leave verses to the boys at school,* &c., is out of place. Poetry which observes the rules of composition seems as compatible, as prose, with mental harmony.

l. 218. *When golden angels cease to cure the evil,* &c. The antithesis here is between disbelief in the efficacy of touching for the King's Evil, and belief in the flattery of servile chaplains. But it is so obscurely put as to be barely intelligible, and the only excuse that can be offered is, that the original lines in Horace are no less awkward than the imitation.

the evil. Scrofula, popularly called the King's Evil. It was a part of the Jacobite creed that the power of curing the Evil by touch was possessed by the exiled Stuarts, but not by the House of Hanover. Carte, the Jacobite historian, embodied the belief in his History of England. It had not died out in Scotland in 1745, when Prince Charles Edward touched a child at Holyrood.

l. 220. The persons here meant are White Kennet, afterwards Bishop of Peterborough, and the Duke of Devonshire. The sermon alluded to was preached by Kennet, the Chaplain, at the funeral of the first Duke. The sermon made a great noise at the time, and was much ridiculed by the wits. Among others, Dr. King of Dublin wrote a *jeu d'esprit*, a refutation of a sermon of Clemens of Alexandria on the text, 'How hardly shall they that have riches enter into the kingdom of heaven.' As the sermon was preached as far back as 1707, and Dr. Kennet had died in 1728, the allusion must have been unintelligible to most of Pope's readers, in 1737. But it is revived by Pope in order to direct a brutal insult against the third Duke, then living, an amiable and accomplished nobleman, whose unpardonable crime was that of having accepted the office of High

Steward on the dismissal of Lord Chesterfield in 1733. The blank in i. 222 is to be filled with the word *Duke*, as Bennett suggested, not with *Dean*, as the editor of Dr. King's Works (1786) has it.

l. 234. *Worldly*, i.e. Edward *Wortley* Montagu. Cf. Sat. and Ep. 2. 49, note.

l. 245. *Half that the dev'l o'erlooks from Lincoln town.* Alluding to the proverb, 'The devil looks over Lincoln.' Fuller (Worthies, vol. 2. p. 6) fancifully explains it of 'the ill aspects of malevolent spectators . . . as the devil overlooked the cathedral of Lincoln, when first finished, with a lowe and tetrick countenance.'

l. 246. *Abhor a perpetuity should stand.* A *perpetuity* in law is the vesting of property to all futurity. Warton, Law Lexicon, s. v.: 'It is odious in law, destructive to the commonwealth, and an impediment to commerce, by restricting the wholesome circulation of property.'

l. 257. *Saperton.* A village about four miles from Lord Bathurst's seat at Oakley, on the road from Cirencester to Stroud. The allusion is to Lord Bathurst's (died 1775) agricultural improvements and inclosures on the Cotswolds. The manor of Saperton was bought from the Atkyns family by Allen Lord Bathurst in 1730. Pope was a frequent visitor at Lord Bathurst's, and in the library at Oakley is a picture in which Pope, Atterbury, Bolingbroke, and Prior are grouped together.

l. 270. *Why, of two brothers, rich and restless one.* Cf. Pers. Sat. 6. 18:
> 'geminos, horoscope, varo
>   Producis genio. . .'

l. 273. *All Townshend's turnips.* Charles, second Viscount Townshend, retired from the Ministry in 1730 in disgust at the growing ascendency of Sir Robert Walpole, whose sister he had married. After his retirement he devoted himself to country pursuits. It is to him that England, and especially his native county of Norfolk, owes the introduction of the turnip from Germany.

all Grovenor's mines. This is the spelling of Warburton's ed. 1751. The proper spelling of the name is now, and was then, Grosvenor. Sir Robert Grosvenor, M.P. for Chester, was the then representative of the family, whose wealth was derived from *mines* of coal.

l. 274. *Why one like Bu—with pay and scorn content.* Bu—is *Bug*, i.e. Lord Hervey. Sat. and Ep. 3. 88. He had voted with the Court ever since the accession of George II. in 1727, and enjoyed a pension of £1000 a-year, before his appointment in 1730 to the office of Vice-Chamberlain.

l. 277. *Oglethorpe.* General Oglethorpe, died 1785, earned commemoration in Pope's gallery of worthies by his Jacobite politics. He was, however, a remarkable man. He first directed attention to the abuses of the London jails. See Epilogue 1. 14, note. His relinquishment of all the attractions

of English life and ample fortune for the settlement of the colony of Georgia
is as romantic a story as that of Bishop Berkeley. Pope's line is valuable as
commemorative of a noble act, though *fly from pole to pole* is a strong
hyperbole for three voyages across the Atlantic. At the time of Pope's
writing he was preparing for his third expedition to Georgia, taking six
hundred emigrants with him. Macaulay mentions (Hist. of England, I. 365)
that Gen. Oglethorpe used to tell that he had shot birds on the site of what
is now Regent-street.

l. 283. *his great end the same. His,* i.e. of the *God of nature.*

l. 287. *would live without a place.* In reading, *would* should be
emphasised.

l. 288. *his favour. His,* i.e. 'the heir's.'

l. 325. Warton remarks that the satire should have ended with this line.
The frigid antithesis in line 327 is not in Pope's manner, and being the last
line leaves behind a false impression of the whole composition.

EPILOGUE TO THE SATIRES.

1738.

DIALOGUE I.

The first Dialogue, under the title of 'One Thousand Seven Hundred and
Thirty-eight,' came out in that year, on the same morning in May as Johnson's London. Though the idea of imitating Juvenal was a plagiarism from
Pope's imitations of Horace, yet the copyist was more vigorous than his master, and London had a more rapid sale than Pope's Dialogue. Macaulay, Life
of Johnson: 'Those small critics who are always desirous to lower established
reputations ran about proclaiming that the anonymous satirist was superior
to Pope, in Pope's own peculiar department of literature. It ought to be remembered to the honour of Pope, that he joined heartily in the applause with
which the appearance of a rival genius was welcomed. He made enquiries
about the author of London. Such a man, he said, could not long be
concealed. The name was soon discovered, and Pope exerted himself to
obtain an academical degree and the mastership of a grammar-school for
the poor young poet. The attempt failed, and Johnson remained a bookseller's hack.'

The Friend is an impersonal interlocutor.

l. 3. *You grow correct, that once with rapture writ.* Here Pope seems to
claim the merit of correctness only for the productions of his age, and to
attribute a higher poetical inspiration to those of his youth. But the account

he gave himself to Spence is the truth. He acted from the very first upon Walsh's suggestion to aim at 'correctness.' See Essay on Man, Introduction.

l. 7. *Horace long before ye said.* See Sat. and Ep. i. 67.

l. 9. *Peter.* See Sat. and Ep. i. 3.

l. 12. *Bubo observes.* Pope's own note on this is, 'Some guilty person, very fond of making such an observation.' We may infer that we have here a favourite remark of Mr. Dodington—'Horace's satire was reserved for follies and foibles, in contradistinction to that of Juvenal, who *lashed vice*.'

l. 13. *Sir Billy.* See below, l. 68.

l. 14. *Blunt.* Sir John Blunt, one of the wealthiest Directors of the South Sea Company. His estate was valued for the liquidation at £183,000.

H—ggins. Huggins had been Warden of the Fleet Prison. He bought the wardenship of Lord Clarendon, the historian, for the sum of £5,000. He made as much per annum by extorting money from the wretched prisoners by ill-usage. This iniquitous system was brought before Parliament by General Oglethorpe; see Sat. and Ep. 6. 277, note, and though it was abated, the miscreants, being tried by a British jury, escaped punishment. A summary of the facts may be read in Wright's Life of Oglethorpe, 1867.

l. 17. *And own the Spaniard did a waggish thing.* Jenkins, master of a trading sloop, who had lost an ear, or part of one, it is not known how, pretended that it had been torn off by a Spanish officer of the customs, who bid him ' carry it to the king his master.' The 'fable of Jenkins' ear,' as Burke, 'Thoughts on a Regicide Peace,' calls' it, produced more effect than anything else in working up the country to take up the cause of the merchants against Spain.

l. 24. *Patriots there are, who wish you'd jest no more.* Pope's own note here is, 'This appellation, *Patriots*, was generally given to those in opposition to the Court. Though some of them, which our author hints at, had views too mean and interested to deserve that name.' Opposite this line Lord Marchmont, Pope's friend and executor, wrote Carteret and Pulteney, intimating that these two, after the Queen's death, were desirous of modifying their opposition to the Court.

l. 26. *The great man.* The familiar term for Sir Robert Walpole.

l. 30. *his happier hour.* Horace Walpole describes the effect on his father of the ministerial struggle, which terminated in 1741, in Sir Robert's retirement; Walpole to Mann, Oct. 19, 1741 : 'He who always was asleep as soon as his head touched the pillow, now never dozes above an hour without waking ; and he who at dinner always forgot that he was minister, and was more gay and thoughtless than all his company, now sits without speaking, and with his eyes fixed for an hour together. Judge if this is the Sir Robert you knew !'

l. 31. *Seen him, uncumber'd with the venal tribe.* Lord Hervey, Mem.

l. 24: 'There never was any minister to whom access was so easy and so frequent, nor whose answers were more explicit. He knew how to oblige when he bestowed, and not to shock when he denied; to govern without oppressing, and conquer without triumph.'

l. 34. *He does not think me what he thinks mankind.* Macaulay, Essays, i. 274: 'Sir Robert said after his fall that it was a dangerous thing to be a minister; that there were few minds which would not be injured by the constant spectacle of meanness and depravity.'

l. 37. *with Scripture still you may be free.* The innuendo is intended to be applied, by the reader, to the style of conversation prevalent at Court in the lifetime of Queen Caroline, who died November, 1737.

l. 38. *A horse-laugh, if you please, at honesty.* Pope's own note speaks of 'the laugh here described of ONE who bestowed it equally upon religion and honesty.' Mr. Croker inferred from the capital letters that the Queen was meant. But it seems rather, so far as such an allusion admits of being interpreted, to be aimed at Lord Hervey.

l. 46. *His prince.* At this date the Prince being in violent opposition to the Court, Pope was disposed to be complimentary. Glover, the poet, told Warton of a visit paid by Frederick to Twickenham, when Lyttelton asked Pope to join him in dissuading the Prince from riding a vicious horse. 'I hope, Sir,' said Pope, 'the people of England will not be made miserable by a second horse.'

l. 47. *Lyttelton.* When the Prince discarded Dodington in 1734, Mr. (afterwards Sir George, and Lord) Lyttelton succeeded to the place of favourite. He was, of all the Prince's friends, the most violent in opposition to the Court—a circumstance which doubtless recommended him to Pope. For a portrait of Lyttelton as he appeared to his enemies, see Lord Hervey, Mem. i. 433.

l. 51. *Sejanus, Wolsey.* In 1st ed. *Ægysthus, Verres.* The Opposition speakers in both Houses ransacked history for the most offensive names to heap upon Sir Robert Walpole. Cf. Sat. and Ep., Epilog. 2. 136:

> 'But pray, when others praise him, do I blame?
> Call Verres, Wolsey, any odious name?'

For Fleury, see Sat. and Ep. 1. 75, note. The comparison to Sejanus was made in a speech, in the Lords, in 1721, by the Duke of Wharton But the object of the invective on that occasion was Stanhope, not Walpole.

l. 64. *distinction:* used here for 'distinctness,' 'discrimination.'

l. 66. *Henley.* A graduate of Cambridge and ordained clergyman of the Church of England, who had set up an Oratory of his own in Newport Market about ten years previously, and attracted crowds to hear him. Cf. Dunciad, 3. 199.

Osborne edited at this time a paper called The London Journal, which Lord Chesterfield says (Common Sense, Oct. 8, 1737) he used to take as a soporific every night, after he was in bed. In the coffee-house slang, the editor as well as his paper went by the name of 'Mother Osborne.'

l. 68. *Y—ung.* Sir William Yonge was so ready a speaker that Sir Robert often, when he did not care to enter early into the debate himself, gave Yonge his notes as the latter came late into the House, from which he could speak admirably and fluently, though he had missed the preceding discussion.

l. 75. *Middleton.* The Life of Cicero, Middleton's principal work, was not published till 1741. He was as yet only known as a writer by fugitive pamphlets, against Bentley, on the Origin of Printing, &c.

Bland. Master of Eton College and friend of Sir Robert Walpole. The point lies in coupling Middleton who was considered a very elegant writer, with Bland who was a very bad writer, with the object of disparaging Middleton. For Middleton was a friend of Lord Hervey.

l. 78. *nation's sense.* Here Pope has again preserved a cant term of the party politics of the time.

l. 80. *Hang the sad verse on Carolina's urn.* Queen Caroline, died Nov. 30, 1737. Lord Stanhope, Hist. of England, 2. 314: 'The death-bed of this high-minded princess was not wholly free from blame, still less from the malignant exaggeration of party. She was accused as implacable in hatred, as refusing her pardon to her son. . . . . "Unforgiving, unforgiven, dies," cries Chesterfield in some powerful lines circulated at the time. With still more bitterness, Pope veils his satire beneath pretended praise.' On the other hand, Sir R. Walpole told Horace, that she sent her forgiveness and her blessing to her worthless son. Horace Walpole's authority for a fact is not very good, but neither Pope nor Chesterfield, where the Queen is concerned, can be relied on.

l. 112. *Who starves a sister, or forswears a debt.* In 1st ed. *who starves a mother*, altered in subsequent editions to *sister*. The alteration suggested town scandal, current at the time, against Lady Mary Wortley Montagu. What little foundation there was for the libellous imputations may be seen in Lord Wharncliffe's edition of Lady Mary's Works, vol. 3, App. p. 432. Pope afterwards (Sat. and Ep., Epilog. 2. 20) pretended that his allusion had not been discovered:

> 'Who starv'd a sister, who forswore a debt,
>   I never nam'd, the Town's enquiring yet.'

l. 114. *the dignity of vice.* Cf. Juvenal, 11. 174:

> 'Namque ibi fortunæ veniam damus. Alea turpis,
>   Turpe et adulterium mediocribus; hæc eadem illi
>   Omnia cum faciant, hilares nitidique vocantur.'

Gifford compares Beaumont, Maid in the Mill:

> 'In lords a wildness is a noble trick,
>   And cherish'd in them, and all men must love it.'

l. 123. *Blount.* Charles Blount, younger son of Sir Henry Blount of Tittenhanger. He was one of the earliest of the deistical writers. He committed suicide in 1693.

l. 124. *Passeran.* Alberto Radicati, Conte de Passerani, a Piedmontese nobleman. He resided some time in England. The allusion in Pope's line is to his 'Dissertation sur la Mort,' Rotterdam, 1733, in which he is said to have attempted a justification of suicide.

l. 125.   *But shall a printer, weary of his life,*
        Learn, from their books, to hang himself and wife?

Warton refers to the Gentleman's Magazine, 1732, for an account of the suicide of Richard Smith, a bookbinder.

l. 131. *modest Foster.* Dr. James Foster, a Nonconformist preacher of great popularity in the city of London. The Sunday evening lecture, begun in 1728, which he carried on for twenty years at the Old Jewry, was resorted to by persons of every rank, station, and quality.

l. 134. *Llandaffe.* Pope's note on this is, 'a poor bishopric in Wales, as poorly supplied.' The Bishop of Llandaff was Dr. John Harris, who died August 28 in this year. Why Pope thought him worth launching this line at, I have not discovered.

l. 135. *humble Allen.* 'Low-born Allen' in first edition, changed by Pope after he became acquainted with Allen, and had paid him a visit at Prior Park, near Bath, in November, 1741.

l. 144. *Let greatness own her, and she's mean no more.* Gibbon, ch. 40: 'Without Warburton's critical telescope I should never have seen, in this general picture of triumphant vice, any personal allusion to Theodora.' We are to infer from Warburton's note on the line that Pope owned the allusion to the Empress Theodora. But it is possible that Warburton first suggested it to the poet. The mention of 'old England's genius,' l. 152, seems scarcely reconcilable with Warburton's interpretation. It may with more probability be conjectured that this lofty declamation, which is in the tone of the Craftsman, personifies Sir Robert Walpole's administration as *triumphant vice.*

DIALOGUE II.

1738.

l. 1. *Paxton.* Solicitor to the Treasury: see below, l. 141, 'When Paxton gives him double pots and pay.'

l. 2. *Not yet, my friend! to-morrow 'faith it may.* Alluding to Walpole's Playhouse Act. The effect of this Act was to legalise the Lord Chamberlain's customary power of licensing plays. The opposition affected to think that this was only a first step towards the establishment of a censorship of the Press. Lord Chesterfield delivered, June 2, 1737, a brilliant harangue urging this argument. The speech is in print, in his Works, vol. 5. p. 2.

l. 11. *Guthry.* Pope, note: 'The Ordinary of Newgate, who published the Memoirs of the malefactors, and is often prevailed upon to be so tender of their reputation, as to set down no more than the initials of their names.'

l. 20. *Who starv'd a sister, who forswore a debt.* See above, Sat. and Ep., Epilogue 1. 112, note.

l. 22. *The poisoning dame.* Bennett; 'Lady Betty Molineux, who married Dr. St. André, after poisoning her former husband, the friend of Locke.'

l. 31. *beasts of nature,* = 'feræ naturæ.' Pope seems to have taken 'feræ' as a nominative. It is a genitive, and is opposed to 'domitæ naturæ.'

l. 39. *wretched Wild.* Jonathan Wild, hanged in 1725. His Life by Fielding is a romance, or rather a satire on 'greatness.' It was probably suggested to Fielding by an obscure pamphlet, entitled the Life and Glorious Actions of Jonathan Wilde, 1725.

l. 49. *plums.* Cf. Sat. and Ep. 1. 103.

l. 66. *Esher's peaceful grove.* Cardinal Wolsey's house, or what remained of it, was bought by Henry Pelham in 1729. Cf. Thomson, Summer:

> 'To Clermont's terrass'd height, and Esher's groves,
> Where in the sweetest solitude, embrac'd
> By the soft windings of the silent Mole,
> From courts and senates Pelham finds repose.'

This is the passage referred to by Mason, Heroic Epistle, l. 35:

> 'There was a time, in Esher's peaceful grove,
> When Kent and Nature vied for Pelham's love,
> That Pope beheld them with auspicious smile,
> And own'd that beauty blest their mutual toil.'

l. 69. *Craggs.* Sat. and Ep. 4. 45.

l. 71. *Rundel.* Thomas Rundle, Bishop of Derry 1735-1743. Rundle was, like Secker and Butler, patronised by Talbot, Bishop of Durham 1721–1730; but having been connected with Whiston and Clarke, he was suspected of unsound opinions, and Gibson, Bishop of London, stopped his promotion to the bishopric of Gloucester, but compromised with the Queen for an Irish bishopric.

l. 72. *Benson.* Martin Benson, Bishop of Gloucester, 1735-1752.

l. 73. *Berkley.* George Berkeley, Bishop of Cloyne, 1734-1753. Warburton's comment here affords a signal instance of his want of penetration in that subject which he considered more peculiarly his own. He says: 'How his metaphysics came to get him the character of a great genius, I am at a loss to conceive. His pretended demonstration . . being the poorest, lowest, and most miserable of all sophisms, i. e. a sophism which begs the question, as the late Mr. Baxter has clearly shewn; a few pages of whose reasoning have not only more sense and substance than all the elegant discourses of Dr. Berkley, but infinitely better entitle him to the character of a great genius.'

l. 77. *Somers.* Cf. Sat. and Ep., Prol. 139.

l. 79. *Shrewsbury.* Charles Talbot, Duke of Shrewsbury, died 1718. He was Lord High Treasurer in 1714, being at the same time Lord Lieutenant of Ireland.

Carleton. Henry Boyle, Lord Carleton, nephew of the famous Robert Boyle.

l. 80. *Stanhope.* On James, Viscount Stanhope, First Lord of the Treasury in the reign of George I., see Lord Stanhope's History of England, vol. 1. ch. 4.

l. 82. *Atterbury.* Francis Atterbury, Bishop of Rochester, was arrested in 1722, and confined for more than six months in the Tower, without being brought to trial. Though it was known he had been in correspondence with the Pretender, evidence could not be got to criminate him. At last he was proceeded against by a Bill of Pains and Penalties, which deprived him of his preferment, and banished him during life. He went to France, and immediately entered the Pretender's service. See Perry, Hist. of the Church of England, ch. 40.

softer hour. This expression conveys the contrast between the vehemence of Atterbury's public conduct and language and the gentleness of his manners when in the company of his friends, which, says Macaulay (Life of Atterbury, p. 18), 'was such as seemed hardly credible to those who knew him only by his writings and speeches.'

l. 83. *How shin'd the soul unconquer'd in the Tow'r.* Wakefield compares Cowley, 'On the Bishop of Lincoln:'

'Your soul then most shew'd her unconquer'd power,
Was stronger and more armed than the Tower.'

l. 86. *Argyll, the State's whole thunder born to wield.* John, second
Duke of Argyll, born 1678. He perhaps owed this commemoration at
Pope's hands to his desertion of Sir R. Walpole and the Whig party, which
was impending at this date. Warton, however, has preserved a tradition
that he declared in the House of Lords, on occasion of one of Pope's
satires, that if any man dared to use his name in an invective, he would run
him through the body, and throw himself on the mercy of his peers, who,
he trusted, would weigh the provocation. Argyll is apostrophised by
Thomson, Autumn, 929, in the style of hyperbolical panegyric, which was
then thought proper for poetry:

> 'In thee . . . . sees
>   Her every virtue, every grace combin'd,
>   Her genius, wisdom, her engaging turn,' &c., &c.

The omitted stanza in Shenstone's Schoolmistress was a compliment to this
Duke of Argyll. He died 1743.

l. 87. *And shake alike the senate and the field.* Alluding to his gallantry
in Marlborough's campaigns, especially at Malplaquet, where (Smollett,
Hist. of England, 10) 'he distinguished himself by extraordinary feats of
valour; several musket-balls penetrated his clothes, his hat, and periwig.'

l. 89. *The master of our passions, and his own.* According to Lord
Hervey's caustic, but just, appreciation (Memoirs, 1. 28), temper was the one
point in which Sir W. Wyndham had a superiority over Pulteney.

l. 92. *And if yet higher the proud list should end.* A graceful allusion to
his acquaintance with the Prince of Wales. See Sat. and Ep., Epilog. 1. 46,
note.

l. 93. Pope to Swift, 17 May, 1739: 'The Prince shews me a
distinction beyond any merit or pretence on my part; and I have received
a present from him of some marble heads of poets for my library, and
urns for my garden.'

l. 111. *The number.* A classicism; Gr. ἀριθμὸς, Lat. *numerus*, those
who count as population and nothing beyond; the proletariate. See passages
collected by Orelli, Hor. 1 Ep. 2. 27.

l. 116. *What Richelieu wanted, Louis scarce could gain*, i.e. a poet to
celebrate their actions.

l. 120. *To Cato, Virgil paid one honest line :* viz. Æn. 8. 670:

> 'Secretosque pios, his dantem jura Catonem.'

The younger Cato, singularly called 'of Utica' from the place of his death
The force of the words *honest line* lies in the consideration that Virgil
ventured on this allusion to a republican, in the court of Augustus.

l. 129. *Spirit of Arnall! aid me while I lie.* A hack writer for Sir R.
Walpole. He is said (Pope, Dunciad, 2, 315, note) to have received 11,000*l.*
in four years for his political articles in the Free Briton and other papers.

Stanhope, Hist. of England, ch. 18 : 'Sir R. Walpole hired his writers as he would his ditchers, holding no personal communication with them, but placing them under Paxton, Solicitor to the Treasury, or other ministerial subalterns ; persons who in general have more ignorance of, and contempt for, literature, than any other class of gentlemen.'

l. 130. *Polwarth is a slave.* Hugh, Lord Polwarth, third son of Lord Marchmont, came into Parliament in 1734 for Berwick. He was one of the best speakers of the Opposition. Sir Robert used to say, 'When I have answered Sir John Barnard and Lord Polwarth, I think I have concluded the debate.'

l. 133. *Sir Robert's mighty dull.* Ironical; see above, Sat. and Ep., Epil. 1. 34, note.

l. 143. *To break my windows if I treat a friend.* Warton has recorded that this actually happened when Lords Bathurst and Bolingbroke were one day dining with Pope at Twickenham.

l. 150. *Turenne.* See Essay on Man, 4. 100, note.

l. 158. *S—k.* Thomas Sherlock, Bishop of Salisbury.

l. 159. *P—e.* Judge Page. Sat. and Ep. 1. 82, note.

l. 160. *the bard whose distich all commend.* Bubb Dodington again, in a Poetical Epistle to Sir R. Walpole.

l. 164. *be-dropt.* Milton, P. L. 10. 527 :

> 'The soil be-dropt with blood of Gorgon.'

The priest whose flattery be-dropt the crown. Pope's own note is, 'Spoken not of any particular priest, but of many priests.' But Warton affirms it to have been aimed at Dr. Alured Clarke, afterwards Dean of Exeter, who published in this year (1738) an Essay on the Character of Queen Caroline.

l. 166. *florid youth;* ironical allusion to the unnatural paleness of Lord Hervey's complexion.

l. 167. *Whose speech you took, and gave it to a friend.* See Sat. and Ep., Epil. 1. 71; the reference is to Lord Hervey.

l. 172. *As hog to hog in huts of Westphaly.* Westphalia is to this day celebrated for the breeding of swine. The hogs, however, no longer occupy a part of the one room which formed the primitive model of the farm-house. Crabb Robinson, Diary, 1. 70 : 'At one corner the fire, here the beds, there the piggery, and a good carriage-way all through' (1800).

l. 209. *Men not afraid of God, afraid of me.* Wakefield compares Boileau, Discours au Roi, 99 : 'Leur cœur. . . S'il se moque de Dieu, craint Tartuffe et Molière.' But Épître 3 seems more likely to have been Pope's original :

> 'Mais de ses faux amis il craint la raillerie
> Et ne brave ainsi Dieu que par poltronnerie.'

The original of Boileau is Montaigne, Essais, 2. 18 : ' Que peult on imaginer plus vilain, que d'estre couart à l'endroict des hommes, et brave à l'endroict de Dieu ? ' Montaigne refers to ' un ancien ' as having said that to lie ' c'est donner tesmoignage de méspriser Dieu, et quand et quand de craindre des hommes.' The reference is to Plutarch, Lysander, c. 4.

l. 223. *them.* Warburton and all editions, *you*; perhaps an error of the press.

l. 228.   *When black ambition stains a public cause,*
         A monarch's sword when mad vain-glory draws.
Pope in a note tells us that these lines were meant of Cromwell and Louis XIV. The note is confirmatory of the conjecture that even in remarks which are general in form, Pope always had some particular case in mind.

l. 230. *Waller's wreath,* i.e. Waller's ' Panegyric to my Lord Protector,' 1654. In 1660 he addressed a poem ' To the King upon his majesty's happy return.' The congratulation was considered inferior to the panegyric. When Charles told Waller of the disparity, he replied, ' Poets, Sir, succeed better in fiction than in truth.'

l. 231. *Nor Boileau turn the feather to a star.* In his ode on the taking of Namur, Boileau, too ready to prostitute his pen to flattery, had made the white plume worn by Louis XIV. into a star, ' et qui est en effet une espèce de comète, fatale à nos ennemis.'

l. 234. *And opes the temple of eternity.* Wakefield compares Milton, Comus, 13 :

         ' . . . that golden key
       That opes the palace of eternity.'

l. 238. Bennett filled up the blanks in this line with the names *Kent* and *Grafton*, on what authority I know not. But if Lord Marchmont had written in his copy *George* and *Frederick*, as Mr. Carruthers says, it may be considered as Pope's own interpretation of his blanks.

l. 240. *Hough's unsully'd mitre.* Dr. John Hough, who as President of Magdalen resisted James II., survived till 1743, when he died, aged 92, after an episcopate of 53 years.

l. 249. *When truth stands trembling on the edge of law.* The allusion is to the censorship of the Press, which the Opposition affected to believe was designed to be introduced by the Government. Wakefield explains : ' When truth is in danger of being cut by the edge of legal resentment sharply whetted against the satirist, who has the boldness to assert her cause.'

l. 254. *end what you began.* The Essay on Man, as it now stands, is only a fragment of a much larger work, of which the four Epistles were to have formed the First Book.